Immune Morphologies: Forms of Militarization and Alliance in Emergency Processes

Edited by
Chiara Davino and
Lorenza Villani

Published by
Adriatico Book Club

PREFACE

On the evening of February 22, 2020 the national television networks broadcasted a press conference held by the Italian President of the Council of Minister Giuseppe Conte, the Minister of Health Roberto Speranza, the head of the Civil Protection Department Angelo Borelli and the president of the Istituto Superiore di Sanità (Italian National Institute of Health) Silvio Brusaferro. In this conference they announced the enactment of a further law decree for the protection of public health against the spread of the COVID-19 virus.

Cautionary measures had already been implemented in the Veneto region, in the Vo' Euganeo municipality, and the Lodi area of the Lombardy region. However, on February 22, the restrictions became harsher, a second COVID-related death was registered, the number of cases in Lombardy kept rising and, through the live broadcast, the emergency took on a national character.

On the same day we were holding a conference in Perugia, Italy, to present our master's dissertation project, *PANICO. Letture di campi post 11 settembre (Panic. Readings of camps after 09/11)*, discussed almost a year before in March 2019 at Iuav University of Venice. The audience in front of us had been halved by—ironically—that very *panic* which had already been spreading even outside of the areas where there had been outbreaks. It felt surreal to be presenting, on that same afternoon and for the first time in what was not an academic context, the analyses and theses of a research which investigated the normalization of a state of emergency and the phobic fear of the *other*. Everything we had been studying for two years in the framework of migrations and terrorism, was taking shape in a very clear, inter-scalar and transversal way within a *new* context, that of healthcare.

Until that point the starting year of our research had been 2001, with the spread of securitarian and preventive systems on a global scale according to a perceived threat felt towards the *other than self*. After the day of the conference we realized that 2020 would become as relevant as 2001. The *bordering processes* along the national borders and the biological bodies were strengthening systemically and moreover, new securitarian reasons were emerging alongside the usual ones.

To reason in depth about 2020, over the course of 2020 itself, was thus not a *new beginning* but rather the natural development of our research project, with the goal of attempting to keep together the complexity of today's heterogeneous crises and the ensuing *bordering* processes. The idea of a book which holds together different subject areas and experiences comes from this will, allowing us to analyze on several levels the critical issues and possibilities that have emerged since 2020.

INTRODUCTION

The clear concatenation of present-day crises, the predominance of a defensive idea when security is talked about, the use of illness in the political discourse to justify more or less authoritarian and more or less repressive measures, the increased control of bodies and violence along the borders, the marginalization of certain social groups also as a function of the often conflicted relationship between risk exposure and class, the diversified right to im-mobility and the shutdown or selective canalization of mobility according to ethnicity, class, citizenship or occupation, the power of communication in the creation of precise collective imaginaries, the forms of physical or virtual habitation of the planet, the present as a part of broad temporal and geographical trajectories, the relationship between environment and the deep consequences of urbanization, the necessity of a socio-ecological perspective. This is the complex picture that emerged in 2020 through the pandemic spread of a pathogen. In this sense, COVID-19 has played the role of a sensor to evaluate the evolution of spatial and social processes that came before it. And if on one side the global geographies of inclusion and exclusion as a function of a further, health-related risk become more complicated, at the same time there is a necessity to create forms of habitation of the planet based on the creation of new alliances and practices of *de-estrangement*, starting from the indispensable correlation between human and non-human species.

What ties these two aspects together—the polarizing geographies and a new form of *dwelling*—is the concept of *immunity*: a biological function once intended as a junction between the self and the other, which can incorporate the external body in a way that makes its presence acceptable. This concept, however, has taken throughout the centuries an aggressive-defensive connotation that has been used, within a securitarian reality, to organize the relationships with everything that is external. In an age dominated by a *patchy* capitalism, in which precariousness is the norm, and by an anthropocentric vision which produces drastic polarizations, the immune morphologies take the shape of ever new distances,

the repercussions of which are identified in the atomization of society, in practices which always tend to exclude certain
human and non-human groups, and in military dynamics which catch on both at an
institutional level and that of civil society.
To reverse these distances into new alliances, human and multi-species, is for us
the collective goal of the foreseeable future.
Not only, through a re-balance of the *biological* and *biographical* dimensions—one
able to put mankind back into a long list of
living beings, thus deposing it from the role,
according to the other dimension, of exceptional living being in its logical-linguistic
capacity—but also, through an action aimed
at caring for and taking responsibility of the
other, which would allow a real evaluation
of the consequences of one's actions.

We chose to investigate the concept of immunity by combining several voices and focusing
on how this concept is spatialized along
European terrestrial and maritime borders,
on how the immune mythologies act at a
social level and how it could be possible to
deactivate them.

In the first chapter the SARS-CoV-2 virus
is inserted in a complex emergency process,
made up of heterogeneous and nesting crises
which consolidate and perpetuate each other,

structuring today's normalized state of emergency and exception.

Starting from the concept of immunity we thus investigate the relationship between nature and culture through the analysis of polarizing immune geographies. These, across often militarized opposing distances, hierarchize Western society especially when it comes to mobility, or *im-mobility*. The resulting political order, of a securitarian and preventative nature, acts through thought and action paradigms which blur the line between civilian and military spheres; moreover, the continuous criminalization of *otherness* (ab-normal, a-political, *infected*) allows for the legitimization of the presence of omnipresent and inter-scalar borders. Within this differential regime of im-mobility, the *banopticon* dispositif is representative, a manifestation of the widespread network of securitarian practices.

Through an analysis of the physical and virtual securitarian systems active along the internal and external borders of the Schengen Area and the waters of the Mediterranean, we argue how in recent years, and especially during the SARS-CoV-2 emergency, there has been an activation of still-active processes of socio-spatial immunization aimed at defending a political (healthy) *us* against a-political (infected) *others*. The analysis of the amendments made within the Schengen Area to reintroduce border controls, which temporarily discontinue the directives of the acquis, shows the nesting nature of today's crises: the discontinuation of free movement between countries is driven by public health reasons which however overlap with ever more diversified and potential threats (among which, mostly, migratory flows and terrorism). Similarly, the for years ongoing militarization along the Mediterranean frontier, designed to defend the maritime European border from *illegal* migratory flows is escalating according to a health risk which, together with a sophisticated communication system, allows for the transformation of the *war* against the virus into a broader war against human otherness.

Starting from two opposite interpretations, the virus as a *quasi-object*, that is a link of an uninterrupted chain of several natural/cultural factors, even spatially and temporarily far from each other, and the virus as a *mythology*, i.e., as the rhetorical, semiotic and communicative product of the mechanisms of power, the different resulting socio-spatial consequences are investigated in the second chapter. While the first interpretation sees in the virus the tangible proof of the relationships which connect nature and society together, highlighting its *constructive* character in matters of relationships and inter-subjectivity, the latter is significantly anthropocentric and instrumentalizes everything that is different from the self for political ends, through recurring thematic repertoires and narrative structures.

The rhetorically decisive step which distorts the idea of immunity (from inclusion of what one would want to exclude, in a form which makes its pathogenic consequences bearable, to ontological incompatibility between the *healthy* self and the *infected* other) is operated by the mythological machine: a conceptual space which acts through languages, narratives, architectures, practices, laws.

Through a comparison between mythopoetic mechanisms and risk formulation, we argue how immunity is the securitarian answer to a risk identified each time in a different subject; a process which continues to shape, since the eighteenth century, the contemporary social space. Specifically, we focus on the mythopoetic processes at work in the pandemic context: the warlike language which permeates today's media coverage and turns the foreigner into an enemy that must be wiped out; the physical distancing and public gathering as iconic spatialities for the political control of bodies; and finally the infodemic as usual practice in an emergency context. In turn we highlight their effects, focusing on the apparently invisible ones on mental health with the aim of demonstrating their profound social impact.

Through allusions to stories about Christian saints, fifteenth century figurative arts, artistic performances and moving images of the Sixties and Eighties, to news events of the Nineties, Malvina Borgherini in the fourth chapter sees the different symbolic senses, materialized in the object-*body*, that made it a catalyst element for the definition of collective identities and the organization of community spaces, reaching through it all the problematization of both these aspects.

In the contemporary pandemic context, in which the body is given countless meanings—from the body as visualization of contagion to the body as a border—and in which power relations and relations of subordinations between bodies are amplified, Borgherini asks the reader to make a conceptual effort to re-frame and re-read the body's meaning in a deeper way. The immunitarian context, never made explicit in the text—and that always sees a contraposition between a self and an other-than-self—is reconstructed through cultural aspects and facts which deal with the relation and reciprocity between bodies well beyond the epidemic context. Going back to the relation between alive and dead bodies, between the idea of death and that of community, between body and space, bodies and bodies as holders of authority, Borgherini brings out how the genesis of the communitarian condition, and as such also the condition of immunity, goes through the assumption of the experience of death; through the practice of defensive actions against another body, socially represented by images and imageries aimed at its stigmatization; by means of symbolic actions and rituals which create a bond and a mutual recognition. This very reciprocity, however, is questioned by the idea of the body as *already given*—and thus solitary, univocal, exposed, produced, reproduced—and consequently, the very concept of community is deeply in crisis.

In the essay written by Elena Giacomelli and Pierluigi Musarò, the focus is on how language and communication can often affect the de-politicization of certain concepts, resulting in a frequently contradictory and profoundly unrealistic representation of the world. Starting therefore from the idea of non-neutrality of language and communication, Giacomelli and Musarò question themselves on the consequences arising from the association of the words "crisis" and "emergency" to long term political events such as climate change and migrations; that is, on the implications of the *framing* operation able to talk about similar processes as unexpected events which necessitate an immediate response.

By seeing language as a strictly binding instrument for the definition of the response adopted to counter a *crisis*, and, more generally, to build a precise representation of the world, what emerges in the pandemic context is a massive use of metaphors able to justify the systemic search for an enemy. A war, a hunt, a fight that can further consolidate, in the already strongly polarized Western society, a definition of "a national *us* as the victim, and contagion as a *threat* coming from outside." This investigation shows how, in the condition of normalized emergency in which we live, the idea of security is nowadays reduced to *control*, and thus associated with repression and surveillance, within a perspective unable to contemplate it as cure, protection and solidarity.

From the aggressive-military distortion of immunity, which as seen so far translates socially into a phobic fear of *contagion* and spatially in the construction of defensive barriers, both material and immaterial, in the last chapter we return to the original idea of immunity as a porous border. A border able to manage and transform the incompatibility of opposite forces, of the self and the other, in complementary forces. In this sense, the individual and collective bodies are places of ongoing definition of the self as a function of the continuous contaminations (alliances) with the external. Referring back to a concept of *cure* as defined by Donna Haraway, and therefore as precondition of a living in the world willing to take responsibility for all the species that inhabit it, we define how today's immune morphologies show us what will have to be the future role of the spatial practice: promoting, and consequently convey, an idea of space that is both broad and inclusive, spatially and temporally, one that is the socio-ecological product of kinships between humans and between humans and non-humans, in which co-existence is the real internalization of the individual and collective responsibilities on both a local and global scale.

Across two conversations, respectively with Serena Dambrosio and Marco Felicioni, and with Piersandra Di Matteo, we wanted to show how an operative and spatial translation of these concepts is possible.

The first conversation is about Assembramenti (public gatherings), a virtual collective which operates in the field of architecture and that, being born during the first Italian national lockdown, is driven by the attempt to profane the immune mythologies and borders, by deconstructing their mechanisms, to restore the profound complexity of today's nesting crises. Assembramenti therefore was not only born at a time in which social atomization, distancing and *closure* at different scales were established in a predominant way, but also pursues a reflection on architecture and on spatial practices in general as cultural phenomena in which the idea of mutual contamination is central, from the subjects to the subject areas. We conversed with Dambrosio and Felicioni on what it means today to *act together* and what doing it in the digital space implies, on what are the urgent needs felt in the spatial debate and on the political role of architects.

In the second conversation, the starting point of the reflection was Atlas of Transition – New Geographies for a Cross-Cultural Europe, a triennial European cooperation project born in 2017 and aimed at the promotion of an intercultural dialogue between European citizens and newcomers. The reflection was on the role of performative arts in the opposition to the social processes of invisibilization and marginalization. Indeed, the project's goal is to oppose the forms of hostility and violence with which the migratory phenomenon is met in European society by promoting social and spatial practices able to create the conditions for a shared living which can reshape the processes of urbanization and the daily experience of the subjects. The relationship between aesthetic and political dimension, the poetry of relationships that is typical of performative arts, capable of deconstructing borders, and the implications of the inability of meeting and appearing in the physical space during the Pandemic are some of the themes discussed with Di Matteo.

Indeed, during the Pandemic the collective appearance of bodies in public assemblies has been denied, or allowed only in a static way by the decrees of the President of the Council of Ministers. The expansion and unforeseeable movement of an open mass has become the rigid order, foreseen and foreseeable, of a closed mass, often not represented by the bodies of the demonstrators but, as in the specific context of the demonstrations by Italian workers, by objects and devices-symbols of the categories involved each time.

Dwelling on the string of separate demonstrations by the various trades, we wish to highlight what to us appeared to be a profound inability to identify, also and above all in a time of emergency, with a unified and compact social body, beyond everyone's own needs and demands. Although the gathering of bodies in the open and public space has always the exercise of a plural right and a way to subtract from forms of precariousness, the parceled gathering for specific fights, each category for itself, did not become a unified and transversal long-term struggle. In this regard, the mutual assumption of responsibility did not take place, and instead, a deep-rooted social categorization, polarization and atomization was seen, with some protests and demonstrations being more visible and others being completely marginalized. This process, albeit older than the Pandemic, has been exacerbated by it, showing the effects of the neoliberal order on the collective conscience.

These same protests by different categories moreover have resonated in online petitions, themselves by different categories, launched simultaneously on several online platforms. Whilst the virtual participation appears indispensable, as we have seen, when other forms are forbidden or heavily curtailed, it is nonetheless necessary to dwell on the type of crowd that, in this case, gathers virtually. What implications does a crowd

composed by mutually anonymous individ-
ual-accounts, whose commitment is often
fast, have in the long term and on the forms
of participation and collective action?

Regarding a blatant social and spatial
de-politicization, a transversal precariousness which accustoms to the insecurity and
immunity paradigm as an oppositional form,
and a subsequent increase in securitarian,
preventative and military systems, we then
reiterate the need, as researchers of space
and social space in a time of nesting crises,
for a reflection on space as the extremely
political expression of mutual responsibilities in a socio-ecological perspective.

Immune Spatialities: Im-Mobility and Securitization of Borders

Chiara Davino, Lorenza Villani

The SARS-CoV-2 emergency showed how contemporary crises can be inserted in a complex network of *processes*, set between nature and society, urban and environment, human and non-human, which reinforce the activation of dynamics of immunity that are increasingly *militarized*.

COVID-19 made clear how the *bordering* processes, constantly reconfiguring themselves, regulate the im-mobility of human and non-human entities regarded as potential threats to the well-being of the Western community which, consequently, establishes itself as a product of the convergence of a risk- and an immunity-society.

The direct consequence of this system is the establishment of securitarian spaces in which emergency and exception act as normal government formulas, by activating militarized immunity processes.

NATURAL/CULTURAL CRISES

The inextricable relationship between *natural* and *cultural* had already emerged in the nineteenth century with the discovery of microbes, through which it was understood how macroscopic actors, such as humans and cities, determined the distribution and organization of microscopic actors and vice versa.

When in 1984 Alexandre Yersin, a pasteurian bacteriologist from Switzerland, discovered the plague bacillus in Hong Kong, he also understood that social organization could provide more or less a fertile ground for the spread of the illness. In a report he wrote that:

> The dwellings inhabited by the lower classes everywhere are infected hovels in which one barely dares to enter and an incredible amount of people gather... The destruction an epidemic can inflict in such conditions is comprehensible, and so are the difficulties encountered in quelling it![1]

Conversely, Yersin pointed out that the Europeans' homes had been barely touched by the plague, despite being themselves subjected to great risk. Studying the habits of the citizens and the distribution of urban infrastructures within the city's different neighborhoods, Yersin understood how the bacteria spread and acted, thus imposing a re-thinking of the socio-spatial fabric.[2]

1   Bruno Latour, *I microbi. Trattato scientifico politico,* trans. Aurelio Notarianni (Roma: Editori Riuniti, 1991), 125. Original edition: *Les Microbes: guerre et paix, suivi de Irréductions* (Paris: La Découverte, 1984).
2   Ibid. 124–132.

Similar dynamics emerge in the same way with the coronavirus. While the idea of COVID-19 acting democratically on the social fabric quickly caught on, it has since become clear that the measures taken to counter its spread have not acted in the same way. Social distancing and quarantine measures have widened pre-existing social inequalities, making the living conditions of some groups untenable. These groups, especially in the socio-urban outskirts, didn't have access to an internet connection, to public transportation, and tend to live in overcrowded dwellings. The virus had therefore a larger impact, even if not on the health, then on the quality of life of some groups. In this sense, the ever-changing relationship between nature and culture ensures that one constantly determines the other and vice versa, consistently shaping society and, more generally, Gaia, intended as a complex system of agencies of the new climate regimen in which in-animate objects and over-animated subjects no longer exist.[3]

The virus, intended as a *super-globalizer*,[4] inserts itself in a complex system of emer-

3   See Bruno Latour, *La sfida di Gaia. Il nuovo regime climatico*, trans. Donatella Caristina (Milano: Meltemi, 2020), 52. Original edition: *Face à Gaïa. Huit conférences sur le nouveau régime climatique* (Paris: La Découverte, 2015).
4   Bruno Latour, "La crisi sanitaria ci induce a prepararci al cambiamento climatico," *Antinomie* (April 1, 2020).

gency in which heterogeneous crises are nesting in each other—economic, health-related, environmental, migration-related. These need to be interpreted as more complex systems which, reciprocally amplifying and perpetuating each other,[5] lead to the normalization of the state of emergency and exception, and the institutionalization of a sense of insecurity on a global scale.[6]

Supplementing this articulated network of natural/cultural crises is a dense system of human interdependencies because of which, as stated by Zygmunt Bauman, everything an individual does or fails to do has more or less a large influence on someone else's prospects and possibilities. In this sense, the Polish sociologist highlights how the ambitions of freedom, security and well-being of a part of the contemporary population are unsuitable to be universally shared and extended.[7] These polarizing natural/cultural morphologies, which put privilege and non-privilege patterns in opposition, enhance the inequalities and legitimize the development and normalization of increasingly sophisticated

5   See Salar Mohandesi, "Crisis of a new type," *Viewpoint Magazine* (May 13, 2020).
6   The term "institutionalization" is meant as the process which consolidates something introducing it into common usage. See Ota De Leonardis, *Le istituzioni* (Roma: Carocci, 2001).
7   See Zygmunt Bauman, *Paura Liquida*, trans. Marco Cupellaro (Roma-Bari: Laterza, 2009), 80–93. Original edition: *Liquid fear* (Cambridge: Polity Press, 2006).

security systems aimed at the *preservation* of precise human groups. These can be defined, within the new global order, as "geo-social" elites, a term which is understood as the new social subdivision based on the level of access each group has to a range of resources such as clean water and air, healthcare, and an internet connection.[8]

The sense of insecurity and addiction to fear in the world's richer and more developed countries, despite their standards of living being the highest ever to be registered in the history of humankind,[9] reinforce pre-emptive, exceptional and immunity-oriented governmental formulas, and therefore a security state.

The "risk society"—as Ulrich Beck calls contemporary society—is therefore *reflexive*, insofar as it generates its own risks.[10] In this

26

8　See Nikolaj Schultz, "Reassembling the Geo-Social: A Conversation with Bruno Latour and Nikolaj Schultz," *Theory, Culture & Society* 36, no. 7–8 (2019): 215–230.

9　According to Robert Castel, for the citizens of developed countries two forms of protection are guaranteed: civil and social. The first includes the fundamental freedoms within the rule of law; the second includes the protection from risks, such as, for example from illness, lack of money during old age, and the contingencies of life. See Robert Castel, *L'insicurezza sociale. Che significa essere protetti?*, trans. Mario Galzigna and Maddalena Mapelli (Torino: Einaudi, 2004), 3. Original edition: *L'insécurité sociale: Qu'est ce qu'être protégé?* (Paris: Seuil et La République des Idées, 2003).

10　See Ulrich Beck, *La società del rischio. Verso una seconda modernità*, trans. Walter Privitera, Carlo Sandrelli, and Melania Mascarino (Roma: Carocci, 2000), 255. Original edition: *Risikogesellschaft. Auf dem Weg in eine andere Moderne* (Frankfurt am Main: Suhrkamp Verlag, 1986).

sense, a greater perception of these risks, in terms of knowledge, is directly proportional to a greater awareness thereof.[11] Although placed between present and foreseeable future, between real and unreal, the risk only has real consequences if a sufficient number of people consider it to be real.[12]

Within this system, every level of security is determined in function of a projected threat, and every political subject to be defended is opposed to another subject—individual, collective or biological—considered to be potentially dangerous, and thus a-political.[13] Viral agents, the threat of terrorism on a global scale stemming from the 9/11 attacks, and migrants to whom the concepts of risk and insecurity are attributed to on a personal level, these are but some of the contemporary a-political subjects equated with risk factors from which society must be defended. The proliferating fear of being *touched by the unknown* is determined by both the growing

---

11   See Niklas Luhmann, *Risk: a sociological theory*, trans. Rhodes Barrett (Berlin: De Gruyter, 1993). Original edition: *Soziologie des Risikos* (Berlin: De Gruyter; New York, 1991).

12   Risk can manifest itself *directly*, with the reproduction, for example via the media, of an event, or *virtually*, and thus in purely imaginary and catastrophic terms. See John Adams, "Risk and morality: three framing devices," in *Risk and morality*, ed. Richard V. Ericson and Aaron Doyle (Toronto: University of Toronto Press, 2003), 87–103.

13   See Andrea Cavalletti, *La città biopolitica. Mitologie della sicurezza* (Milano: Mondadori, 2005), 17–18.

awareness of the risks, and the globalization processes which, by opening borders, also stokes the fear of losing identity.[14] The direct consequence of this is the reinforcement of a regime that revolves around safety, and thus around the totalitarian protection of one's own person and extensions, which in turn legitimizes the creation, on different scales, of militarized distances between spaces, and individual bodies.

IMMUNITY AND ITS SPATIALIZATION

Immunity can be seen both as a junction point between different entities, between self and other, and as a self-preserving mechanism in reaction to a risk, identified in a foreign body. Immunity mechanisms, present in every historical period in the face of an ever-growing production-awareness of risks, have reached their peak in the twenty-first century, taking the shape of militarized processes. Indeed in contemporary society, security measures are not adjusted to the risk level; on the contrary, it is the risk perception that is adjusted to the growing need for

---

14   On the fear of being touched see Elias Canetti, *Massa e potere*, trans. Furio Jesi (Milano: Adelphi, 2015). Original edition: *Masse und Macht* (Hamburg: Verlag Claassen, 1960).

protection—thus turning the *protection* itself into one of the *major risks*.[15] It follows that the immune prerogative of the definition of a healthy self and a potentially infected otherness, is translated in oppositional spatialities. This political order, security- and prevention-related, makes use of medical immunization to activate processes of medicalization—in which medicine goes beyond its therapeutic scope—[16] and, to prevent the *death* of the social body in relation to potential risks, incorporates into itself what it wants to exclude—such as in the case of the state of exception which turns a sudden contingency into a legal fact.

Risk as a governmental paradigm activates *preventive* systems which acquire a spatial asset in which there applies an *extra ordinem* political idea. These spaces, directly created by the state of exception, take, according to Giorgio Agamben, the name of *camps*. In these, the most absolute biopolitical ideal is spatialized, since power, directly relating to biological life without any form of mediation, reduces the individual to the condition of *nuda vita*, for which no right

15   Roberto Esposito, *Immunitas. Protezione e negazione della vita* (Torino: Einaudi, 2002), 16.
16   See Mario Colucci, "Medicalizzazione," *JCOM Journal of Science Communication* 5, no. 1 (Trieste, 2006).

can be representative of its status other than the sole quality left to it, that of being human.[17] These spatialities built to enclose groups of people deemed abnormal, a-political or infected, are juxtaposed to the definition of *refuges*: spaces in which groups of people settle to protect themselves from potential threats.[18]

Within these socio-spatial systems, strictly controlled and separated from each other, immunity takes on a purely privative and circumstantial meaning, constricting the life's body, individual or collective, and preventing and regulating its existence and expansion outside of it.[19]

Modern society is thus the product of the violence of the right, understood as violence for the right to control violence itself, and the immune mechanisms needed for its constraint; in this sense immunization becomes a founding dispositif of Western civilization.[20] The militarization of civil society, a part of the normalized contempo-

---

17   See Giorgio Agamben, *Mezzi senza fine* (Torino: Bollati Boringhieri, 1996).

18   See Chiara Davino and Lorenza Villani, *Panico. Letture di campi post 11 settembre* (La Spezia: Il Filo di Arianna, 2021).

19   The body is intended as the center of the action by a government which, in relation with life, excludes any of its qualitative forms. See Michel Foucault, "La nascita della medicina sociale" (1977), in *Archivio Foucault. Interventi, colloqui, interviste (1961-1985)* 3, ed. Alessandro Pandolfi (Milano: Feltrinelli, 1997)

20   See Roberto Esposito, *Immunitas*, 39.

rary immune regime, results in paradigms of thought, action and politics designed to establish security zones (which re-organize the living space), to spread military ideas of tracing and to define an economy of surveillance and security; conditions which make the border between the civilian and military spheres increasingly blurred. The criminalization of otherness allows for the legitimization of military methods, tactics and technologies which themselves shape the social space, leading to a proliferation of low intensity conflicts and ubiquitous borders within it. These are put up on different scales—body, home, city, nation, cyberspace—against both human and non-human subjects deemed to be potentially *contaminating*. These spatialities of immunity contribute to reasserting a widespread sense of insecurity within the collective conscience, in turn perpetuated by the populace's own actions. An example of this are the anti-terrorism campaigns which exacerbate the sense of fear and the sole prerogative of safety, during the SARS-CoV-2 emergency, which consolidates an already-present *exophobia* (the fear of everything that is external).[21]

---

21   Donatella Di Cesare, *Virus sovrano? L'asfissia capitalistica* (Torino: Bollati Boringhieri, 2020), 23.

The consequence of these conditions, which compel every nation-state to rethink the very concepts of security, defense and internal safety in relation to a new natural/cultural emergency order on a global scale, is the activation of the *banopticon*, a dispositif utilized for the *regulation* of cross-border mobility.[22] The banopticon, which is transversal, fragmented and heterogeneously diffused within society, as opposed to Bentham's panopticon, is the manifestation of a capillary network of security practices. In it, a vast corpus of discourses, institutions, architectures, laws and technologies merge, used to exclude, profile and impede the mobility of groups of people because of their potentially threatening behavior and the risk factor attributed to them.[23]

The banopticon dispositif represents a differential regimen of mobility (called by us "im-mobility") which increases the status inequalities between different geo-social

32

---

22 On the term "banopticon": combination of the terms "ban" and "opticon", following the conceptualizations of respectively Jean-Luc Nancy and Michel Foucault. With the term "ban" Nancy refers to the law's power to effectively exclude someone from itself and thus *abandoning* them. This ban is the law's ability to include the exception in itself; therefore it is literally impossible to say whether the one who was banished, or abandoned, is within the system or not. See *Terror, Insecurity and Liberty. Illiberal practices of liberal regimes after 9/11,* ed. Didier Bigo and Anastassia Tsoukala (New York: Routledge, 2008), 31–33; Giorgio Agamben, *Homo sacer. Il potere sovrano e la nuda vita* (Torino: Einaudi, 1995), 34.

23 See Bigo and Tsoukala, *Terror, Insecurity and Liberty.*

classes and gives rise to a mobility conflict which spatializes especially along border lines between enclaves and refuges, such as in the *Mediterranean enclave*, a militarized liquid frontier, set up to defend the *Schengen security refuge*. In the last few years, and even more during the SARS-CoV-2 emergency, within these two spaces, militarized immune systems aimed to the regulation of im-mobility have been activated, which varying according to the attribution of a risk factor to each body, determine the activation or deactivation of the security systems.

SCHENGEN REFUGE

The Schengen Area, established in 1985, spatializes the member states' ambition of maximum freedom of movement within a security space; a prerogative that, however, is in contrast to the need to meet the contemporary heterogeneous emergencies which are projected in it, and exclude the numerous forms of *otherness* who attempt to access it. In this sense, the theme of migration policies has assumed a central role ever since the Area's establishment, inasmuch the abolition of internal border controls allows for an easier movement of third parties from one state to the next. To address and prevent threats personified in undesirable foreign subjects, the member states adopted an immune-military strategy—even among themselves—of constant re-introduction of internal border controls, with the subsequent suspension of the Schengen acquis' directives—a set of rules and regulations which regulate the relationships between the states who signed the Convention. Article 25 of the Regulation (EU) No 300/2016 indeed establishes that

> The reintroduction of internal border control might exceptionally be necessary in the case of a serious threat to public policy or to internal security at the level of the area without internal border control or at national level, in particular following terrorist incidents or threats, or because of threats posed by organised crime.[24]

Between 2006 and 2018, *extrema ratio* measures have been introduced because of emergencies of an *extremely* heterogeneous nature—primary and secondary migratory flows, terrorism, sport events, international summits, political events. In the last years, however, the number of measures to reintro-

---

24 Regulation (EU) no. 2016/399 of the European Parliament and of the Council of March 9, 2016 on a Union Code on the rules governing the movement of persons across borders (Schengen Borders Code) (2016).

duce internal border controls has gradually increased, and so has the temporal extension of these measures.

Starting in 2015, year in which a large number of dead and missing persons was registered in the Mediterranean basin,[25] the measures adopted towards those who were part of secondary movements took on a punitive nature.[26] Just after the beginning of 2015 there has been a prevalence of measures triggered by migratory flows, regardless of Article 5 of Regulation (EU) No 1051/2013 of the European Parliament and the Council on October 22, 2013, amending Regulation (EC) No 562/2006 in order to provide for common rules on the temporary reintroduction of border control at internal frontiers in exceptional circumstances. This article states that "migration and the crossing of external borders by a large number of third-country nationals should not, per se, be considered to be a threat to public policy or internal security."[27] This condition highlights the normalization of the state of emer-

25 See Davino and Villani, *Panico*.
26 Lorenzo Vianelli, "Proteggere o controllare? Il sistema europeo comune di asilo nello spazio Schengen," *Zapruder*, no. 51 (2020): 34–53.
27 Regulation (EU) no. 1051/2013 of the European Parliament and of the Council of October 22, 2013 amending Regulation (EC) no. 562/2006 in order to provide for common rules on the temporary reintroduction of border control at internal borders in exceptional circumstances (2013).

gency and the subsequent legitimization of military and immune logics to counteract the movement of forms of otherness deemed to be potentially dangerous.

The amendments made to the acquis by the member states during the SARS-CoV-2 emergency show the nesting nature of contemporary crises. Indeed, in addition to the suspension of internal movement to contrast the spread of the virus, since March 2020, controls at the internal borders of the Schengen Area have been reintroduced also to tackle the new potential threats created by the behavioral changes caused by the lockdown, and generally by the Pandemic. For example, since the declaration of "global pandemic" by the World Health Organization in March 2020, the Counter-Terrorism Committee Executive Directorate (CTED) has declared an increase of the threat of terrorism, caused also by the time spent online by mostly students, for whom, in some circumstances, a full-time education was not guaranteed at the time.[28] In view of such a threat, Austria, France, Sweden, Norway and Denmark have reintroduced controls at their borders, adopting and strengthening yet

36

---

28   See CTED, *The impact of COVID-19 on counter terrorism and countering violent extremis* (June 2020).

again preventive, immune and military logic proper to the Schengen securitarian refuge.

On June 5, the reopening of the Schengen borders marked the return to normalcy of a strongly differentiated global mobility regimen, which regulates it according to global geographies of race and class. Indeed, during the Pandemic and more generally throughout the last years, borders have acted as "semi-permeable membranes" for the canalization of motilities, taking the form of interactive architectures which change according to the citizenship of those who try to cross them.

The borders, seen as regulation dispositif between birth and nation—and therefore as bio political architectures—define securitarian spatialities, physical and virtual, designed to exclude the *otherness*.[29] The militarization which in the last decades involved the Mediterranean enclave allows the argument of how immune processes are activated, in this specific case, towards third-party citizens and their movement, classified as *illegal*, also because of the risk factor attributed to them.

29 On the concept of border, seen also as a semi-permeable membrane, see Alessandro Petti, *Arcipelaghi e enclave: architettura dell'ordinamento spaziale contemporaneo* (Milano: Bruno Mondadori, 2007), 6 ; see also Valeska Huber, "The unification of the globe by disease? The international sanitary conferences on cholera, 1851-1894," *The Historical Journal* 49, no. 2 (2006): 453–476.

This categorization allows for the employment of military forces since the end of the 1990s, which, with time and the increase of migratory flows, went from being exceptional to being systematic and on a long-term basis. Likewise the deployment of military forces for the protection of the internal security of member states is incompatible with a threat of a non-military nature—that posed by migration flows—which, *normally*, is met by law enforcement.[30]

This regime results in the activation of military operations in the Mediterranean, and in the development of ever-innovative technologies which, by linking an ever-increasing number of interconnected networks, make the rejection of foreign citizens easier, on the basis of statistical analyses. This double spatiality of immune-military systems, physical and digital, shows the complexity of the practices which take place along the Mediterranean frontier.

30 "The difference is not a negligible one: while both the police and the military are central in upholding state sovereignty, the former would work under a logic of 'minimal force' in normal political circumstances, whereas the latter would work under a logic of 'maximum force' during an emergency, seeking to defeat an enemy". See Agnese Picciardi, "A liquid frontline: new war imaginaries in the Mediterranean Sea," *Security praxis* (April 23, 2020).

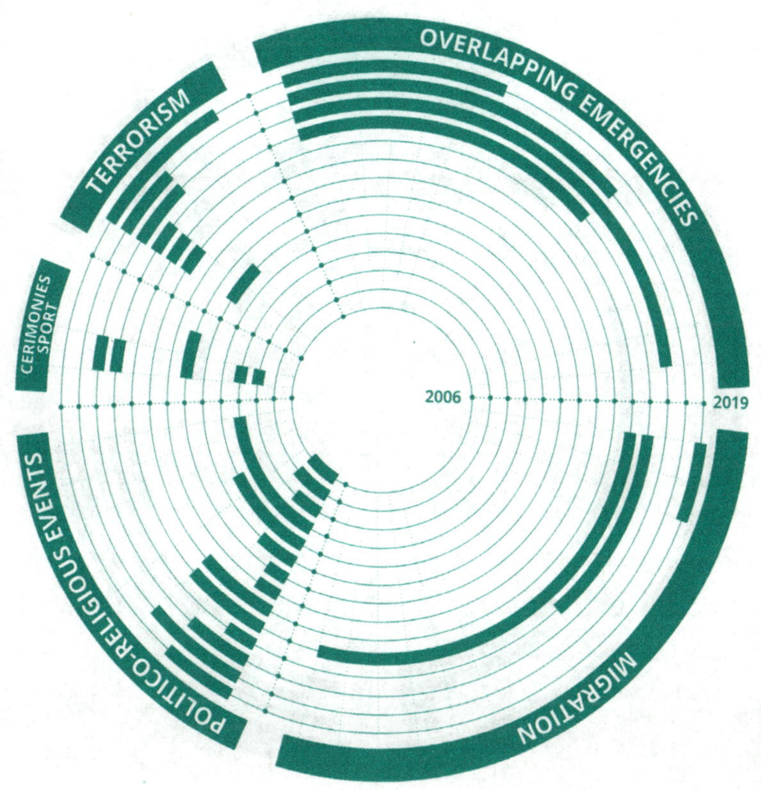
OVERLAPPING EMERGENCIES
TERRORISM
CERIMONIES
SPORT
POLITICO-RELIGIOUS EVENTS
MIGRATION
2006
2019

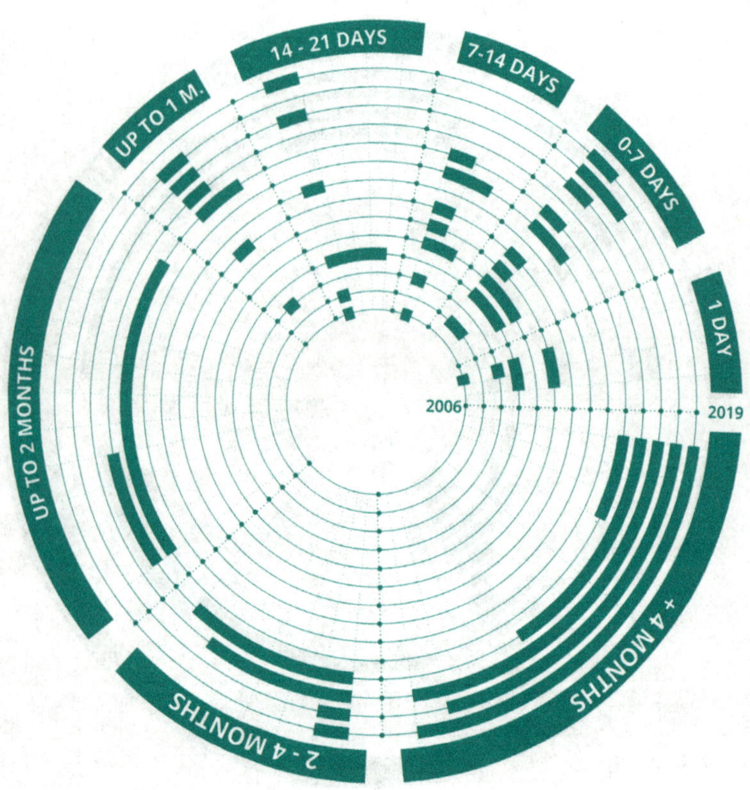

14 - 21 DAYS
7-14 DAYS
UP TO 1 M.
0-7 DAYS
1 DAY
UP TO 2 MONTHS
2006
2019
+ 4 MONTHS
2 - 4 MONTHS

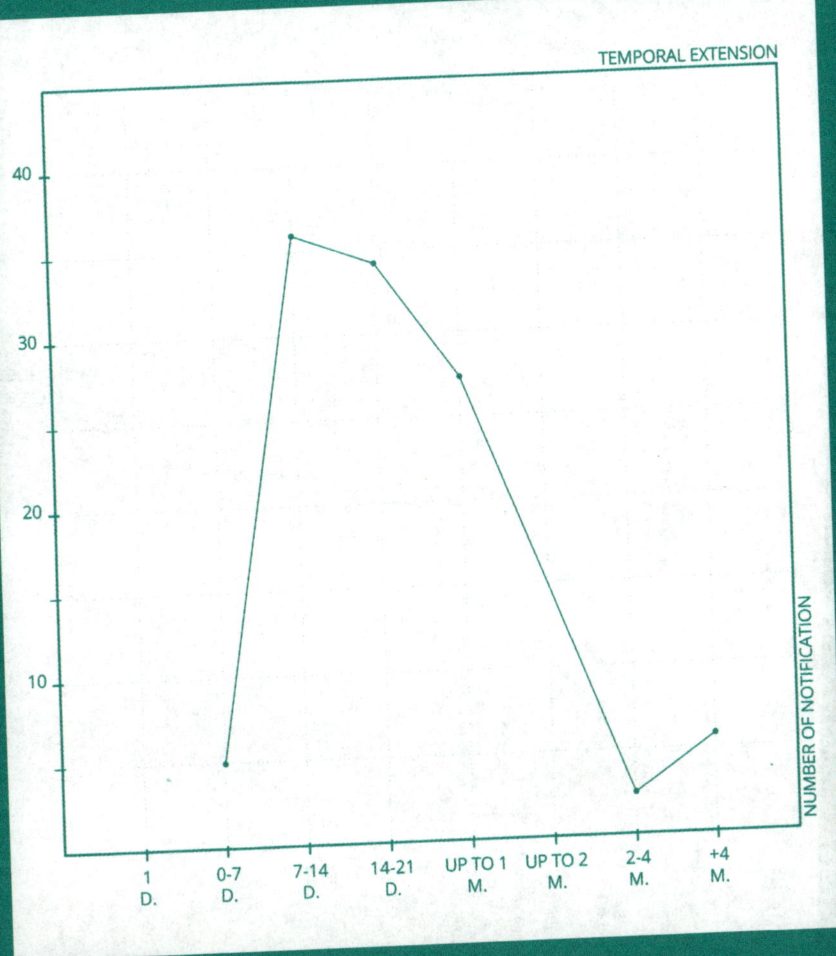

TEMPORAL EXTENSION
NUMBER OF NOTIFICATION
40
30
20
10
1 D.
0-7 D.
7-14 D.
14-21 D.
UP TO 1 M.
UP TO 2 M.
2-4 M.
+4 M.

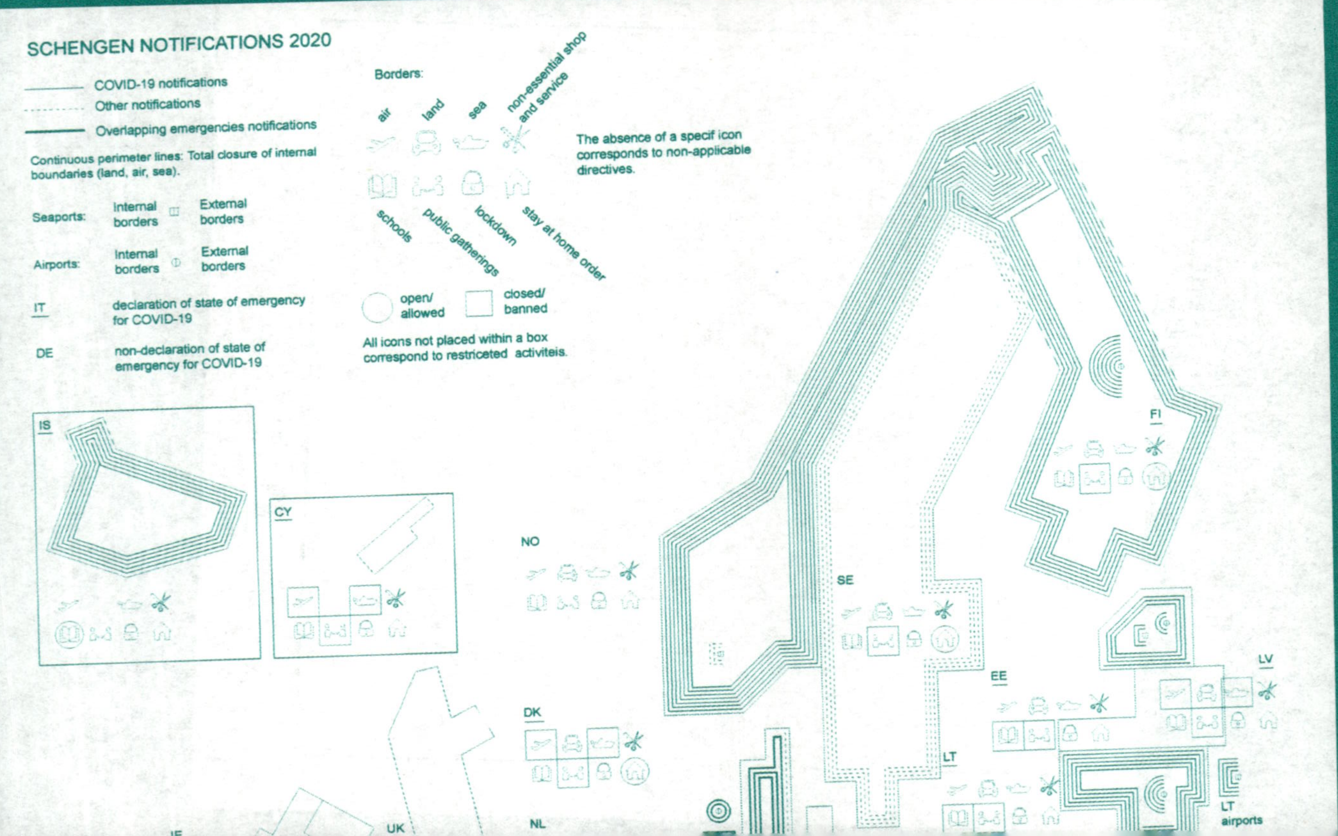

SCHENGEN NOTIFICATIONS 2020
COVID-19 notifications
Other notifications
Overlapping emergencies notifications
Continuous perimeter lines: Total closure of internal boundaries (land, air, sea).
Seaports: Internal borders External borders
Airports: Internal borders External borders
IT declaration of state of emergency for COVID-19
DE non-declaration of state of emergency for COVID-19
Borders:
air land sea non-essential shop and service
schools public gatherings lockdown stay at home order
The absence of a specif icon corresponds to non-applicable directives.
open/ allowed closed/ banned
All icons not placed within a box correspond to restriceted activiteis.
IS
CY
NO
SE
FI
EE
LV
DK
LT
LT airports
NL
UK
IE

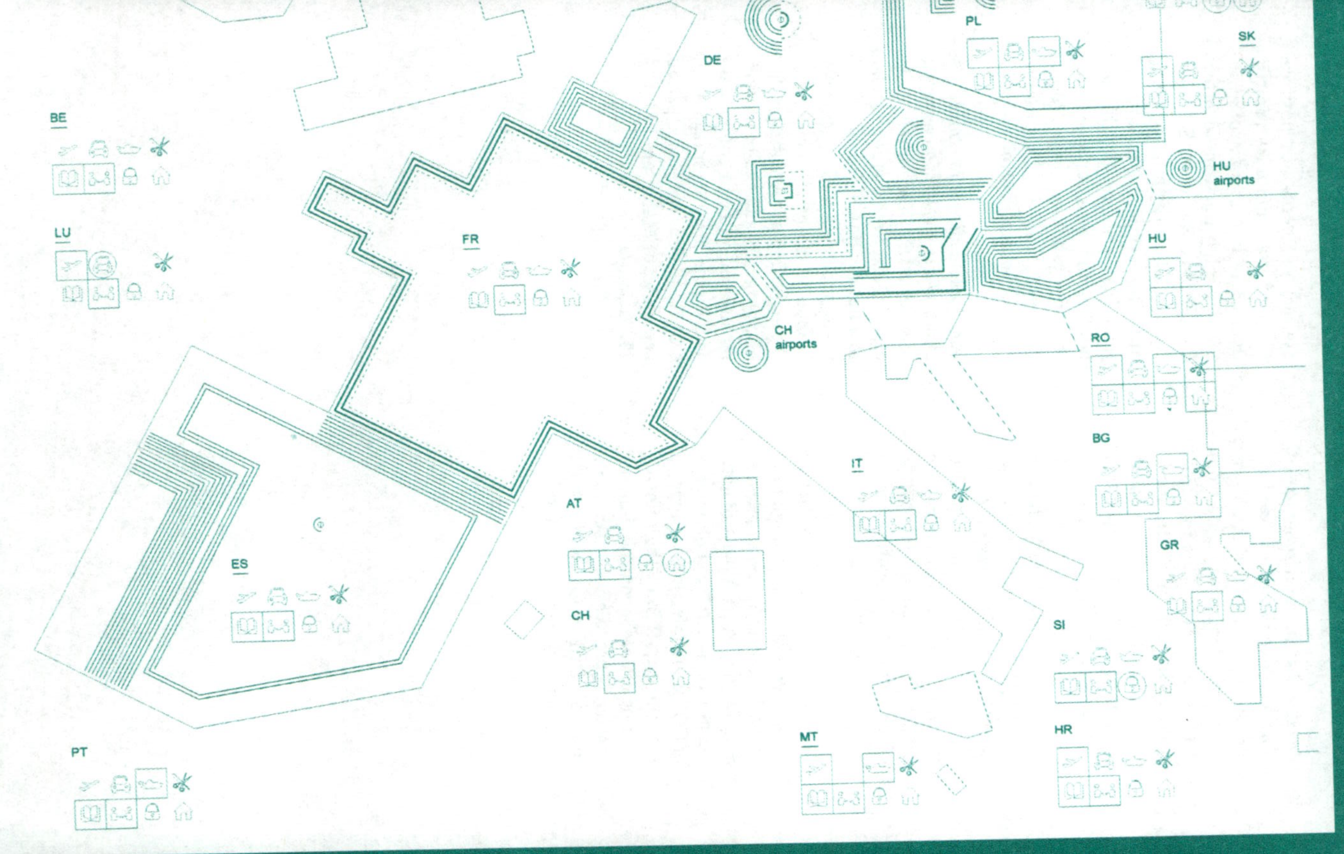

BE
LU
PT
DE
FR
ES
AT
CH
PL
SK
HU airports
HU
RO
BG
IT
GR
SI
HR
MT
CH airports

39   *Reasons for the reintroduction of controls along the internal and external borders of Schengen Member States.* Reference period from 2006 to 2019. From 2016 onwards, controls have been reintroduced for multiple reasons due to emergencies of a different nature that overlap and amplify each other.

40   *Average duration of reintroduction of controls along internal and external borders of Schengen Member States.* Reference period from 2006 to 2019. From 2015 onwards, the average duration of reintroduction of controls has drastically increased compared to previous years.

41   *Average duration of reintroduction of controls along internal and external borders of Schengen Member States during 2020.* Almost all notifications concern the containment of COVID-19 infections; it appears that the duration of the reintroduction of border controls, initially shorter, is progressively increasing towards notifications with a total duration of more than 4 months.

Source: Member States' notifications of the temporary reintroduction of border control at internal borders pursuant to Article 25 and 28 et seq. of the Schengen Borders Code. (https://ec.europa. eu/home-affairs/sites/homeaffairs/files/what-we-do/policies/ borders-and-visas/schengen/reintroduction-border-control/docs/ ms_notifications_-_reintroduction_of_border_control_en.pdf)

42   *Schengen Acquis notifications 2020. Reintroduction of border controls at member states from March to December 2020.* Each line corresponds to a notification. For each state it is also indicated, with specific reference to the health emergency, the activation of the national state of emergency and the limitations imposed on different contexts and activities to limit the spread of the COVID-19 virus (reference period: beginning of March until May 14, 2020). Source: Frontex.

MEDITERRANEAN ENCLAVE

The military and humanitarian operation Mare Nostrum, activated in the central Mediterranean on November 18, 2013 following the October 3 shipwreck off the coast of Lampedusa in which more than 350 people have died, was coordinated solely by the Italian government, without involvement by Frontex, the European agency for the coast- and border guard.

The Marina Militare, the Italian navy, was tasked with both dealing with the increasing number of illegal arrivals and the growing number of deaths due to the shipwrecks. It coordinated the mission together with the Italian Air Force, the Carabinieri, the Coast Guard, customs and regular police, Red Cross and the Order of Malta.

To the defense of Italian and European citizens—the war against the invasion by illegal foreign citizens—a humanitarian side was added, inherent to every situation of conflict—thus saving the *others*, the same foreign citizens.[31] The operation's double character becomes particularly evident in

---

31 See Pierluigi Musarò, "Mare Nostrum: the visual politics of a military-humanitarian operation in the Mediterranean Sea," *Media, Culture & Society* 39, no. 1 (2017): 18.

the visual politics which described it, and which contributed to consolidate the general necessity of a security regime in the waters of the central Mediterranean. In the official video of the operation, shot by the very servicemen and women—*frontline filmmakers*—images of military vehicles alternate with close-ups of rescued women and children, denied, in their representation, of any agency. This sequence shows, on one side, the semblance of a migratory invasion which legitimizes a military response, and on the other, the *humanitarian battlefield*.[32]

The use of images, video and diverse media defines, time after time, the border's conditions of existence and the characters this assumes for the different political subjects which relate to it. Similarly, this emerges in the audio-visual materials produced by Frontex, particularly in those centered on the route towards Europe. The route's violence, stylized through silhouettes and stereotypical representations, *finds a solution* in the military governance along the borders of the Mediterranean, and thus

46

---

32 Marina Militare, "Marina Militare – Video su operazione Mare Nostrum," YouTube video, 3:14, July 25, 2014, https://www.youtube.com/watch?v=H7LWma67WAA ; on the concept of *humanitarian battlefield* see Nicholas De Genova, "Spectacles of migrant 'illegality': the scene of exclusion, the obscene of inclusion, 1914-2012," *Visual Communication* (2013): 315–340.

in the subsequent deportations, via comfortable airplanes, of those who attempted to illegally cross the borders.[33]

Mare Nostrum was replaced on October 31, 2014, by Operation Triton—terminated in February 2018—which, headed by Frontex, had an emblematic role in the definition of an almost exclusively military European management of the Mediterranean migration flows, confirmed and consolidated by the subsequent operations. As declared by the then-executive director of Frontex, Gil Arias,

> This operation [Triton] will be closer to EU shores than Mare Nostrum. [...] In any case, the difference between Mare Nostrum and Triton is fundamentally the nature of the two operations. While Mare Nostrum is clearly a search and rescue operation, Triton will be with a main focus on border control, border management, although as it is obvious saving lives is an absolute priority, and in fact very frequently the control operations, the border control operations coor-

33   Frontex, "Profiting from misery – how smugglers bring people to Europe," YouTube video, 3:09, February 18, 2016, https://www.youtube.com/watch?v=W7OsRz4Ubeg ; Frontex, "The role of Frontex in Return Operations," YouTube video, 1:49, June 23, 2016, https://www.youtube.com/watch?v=O6NO3b6liTs.

dinated by the agency turn into search and rescue operations, and this is how it works in practice.[34]

The European border has progressively moved to the north, matching the Italian territorial waters, consolidating a defensive and security-oriented character. The transition from a humanitarian and military operation to one that is merely military, has been the result of a heated debate which, even today, characterizes the very nature of operations in the Mediterranean.[35]

Indeed, operation Mare Nostrum, both for its range—from Italian territorial waters to those of Libya—and for its substantial monthly cost—nine million euros—was considered by some Italian politicians and by the Frontex Agency itself, a *pull factor* capable of attracting an ever increasing number of migrants along the European coasts and facilitate the work of human traffickers. While the causes for the peaks in arrivals registered during operation Mare Nostrum are to be found in the increas-

48

34   European Parliament, *Hearing of the Committee on Civil Liberties, Justice and Home Affairs (LIBE)*, Multimedia Centre European Parliament (September 4, 2014).
35   For a discussion on the military nature of the last operations in the Mediterranean, see Luca Ceresani, "Operation Irini between arms embargo and migration management," *Security praxis* (May 21, 2020).

ingly violent and unstable conditions of the migrants' countries of origin, the humanitarian aspect has waned in the following operations—as clearly demonstrated by the operations that are currently active.[36] Operation EUNAVFOR MED Sophia (2015–2020) and the one that followed it on March 25, 2020, EUNAVFOR MED Irini—Greek for "wisdom" and "peace" respectively—both active in the central Mediterranean are missions with offensive and coercive mandates (the goal of the former was to gather information to intercept the business models of human traffickers,[37] while the goal of the latter is to enforce the UN arms embargo on Libya).[38]

The militarization underway in the Mediterranean is a political choice which reflects the unwillingness to manage incoming flows in a coordinated and systemic way, on a European level, or to impose a *default* mobility mode which collides with the needs

36 "What emerges from the above is that Mare Nostrum (MN) began operating in the midst of a growing storm, in which the combined exodus of Syrians (and of other nationalities), together with growing instability in transit countries such as Egypt and Libya, and the resulting changing practices of smugglers were leading to record numbers of crossings in increasingly dangerous conditions. Despite the vast resources put in place, MN did not manage to curb the increasing mortality rate at sea. However, it is also clear that MN was not the main cause of this increase". Charles Heller and Lorenzo Pezzani, "Death by rescue," in *Death by rescue* (2016).
37 See Picciardi, "A liquid frontline: new war imaginaries in the Mediterranean Sea".
38 See Ceresani, *Operation Irini.*

triggered by the contemporary geopolitical processes. This policy makes the Mediterranean high seas into a *borderscape* along which the concepts of space, territory, identity and power are reciprocally tied by immunity processes of opposition.

Parallel to the physical border governance, a virtual one exists alongside it, centered on the development of smart controls and analyses of data regarding which people to exclude. According to these, each third party citizen is given a risk factor based on general statistical analyses—not specifically tied to the individual.[39]

These technologies, operating as banopticon dispositif linking an ever-increasing amount of interconnected nets and data, analyze the potentially dangerous behaviors of precise groups in order to build standardized risk profiles that can be applied to every and any third party citizen.

Part of this technological governance is the experimental project iBorder Ctrl, financed by the European Union's Horizon 2020 research and innovation program. The project was launched in September 2016 and finished in August 2019, and was applied for

39 See Didier Bigo, "The (in)securitization practices of the three universes of EU border control: Military/Navy – border guards/police – database analysts," *Security Dialogue* 3, no. 45 (2014): 209–225.

about nine months in specific border crossings outside the Schengen Area—Hungary,
Serbia and Latvia. The project was on a
voluntary basis and involved third party
citizens in a pre-registration to cross over
a Schengen border. In this phase, from
home, the person was required to upload
documents and share data even about their
social media profiles. This data, crossed with
the data banks of different European agencies, allowed the assessment, on the basis of
statistical analyses, of a risk factor for each
individual. The procedure also expected the
third party citizens to answer the question
by the policeman's avatar while being filmed
by their webcam.[40] Through the detection
of micro expressions and thus, the use of
biometric systems, false answers could be
intercepted; these, together with the data
and information apparatus gathered during
the pre-registration procedure, contributed
to establishing the risk factor, and consequently, the amount of controls that the
person would have been subjected to at the
physical border.[41]

40 See Chiara Davino and Lorenza Villani, "La società del controllo. Lettura di spazi
e fatti urbani attraverso il paradigma della trasparenza," *Elephant & Castle*, no. 22
(2020).
41 The information comes directly from the official website of the iBorderCtrl project,
currently unavailable, at the following link https://www.iborderctrl.eu/ (last access
on May 2020).

This evaluation formula for the risk potential, which legitimizes suspicion in function of a categorization structured on previous generalized tendencies, consolidates a preventive regime based on probabilities, and not rights. In this sense, profiling and categorization, in case the data and the documents asked for are not or cannot be submitted or accessed by these third party citizens, they are preemptively excluded.

The militarization of the internal and external borders of the Schengen Area, a result of the adoption of an increasingly *precautionary* government rationale, spatializes an idea of immunity as ontological opposition between *self* and *other than self*. The construction of physical and digital barriers, the deployment of military operations and the development of a vast array of smart border control technologies to better monitor and prevent the movement of the *otherness*, are all emblematic of this government rationale.

During the SARS-CoV-2 pandemic the development of *digital bio-surveillance* systems for the tracing of one's contacts has also involved Europe. While this may seem effective in controlling the virus, it could also reinforce the already well-established tendency to adopt control systems that are increasingly invasive. The introduction of such devices threatens on one hand to transform the body itself into a border, and on the other to legitimize the rejection and the im-mobility of some social groups.

COVID-19, intended as but a piece of a complex net of natural/cultural crises, made the differential im-mobility systems even more evident and sharp, even as a function of the new prerogative of allowing the movement of citizens from countries which have similar risk profiles, when it comes to viral infectiveness.

Health is thus added to the risk factors attributed to precise social groups. This legitimizes on one hand the exclusion of the *foreigner* identified as a potential infection source, and on the other consolidates the adoption of military measures for the rejection of people along the borders, making the war against the non-human virus a war against human *otherness*.

The military assets and armed forces deployed in operations currently active in the Mediterranean

Numbers refer to the total number of vehicles and personnel deployed in each operation

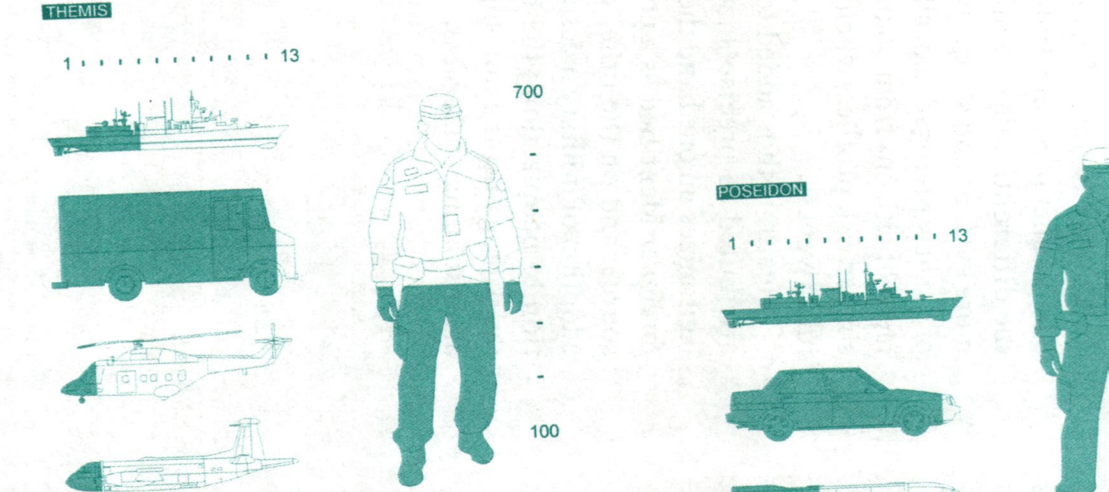

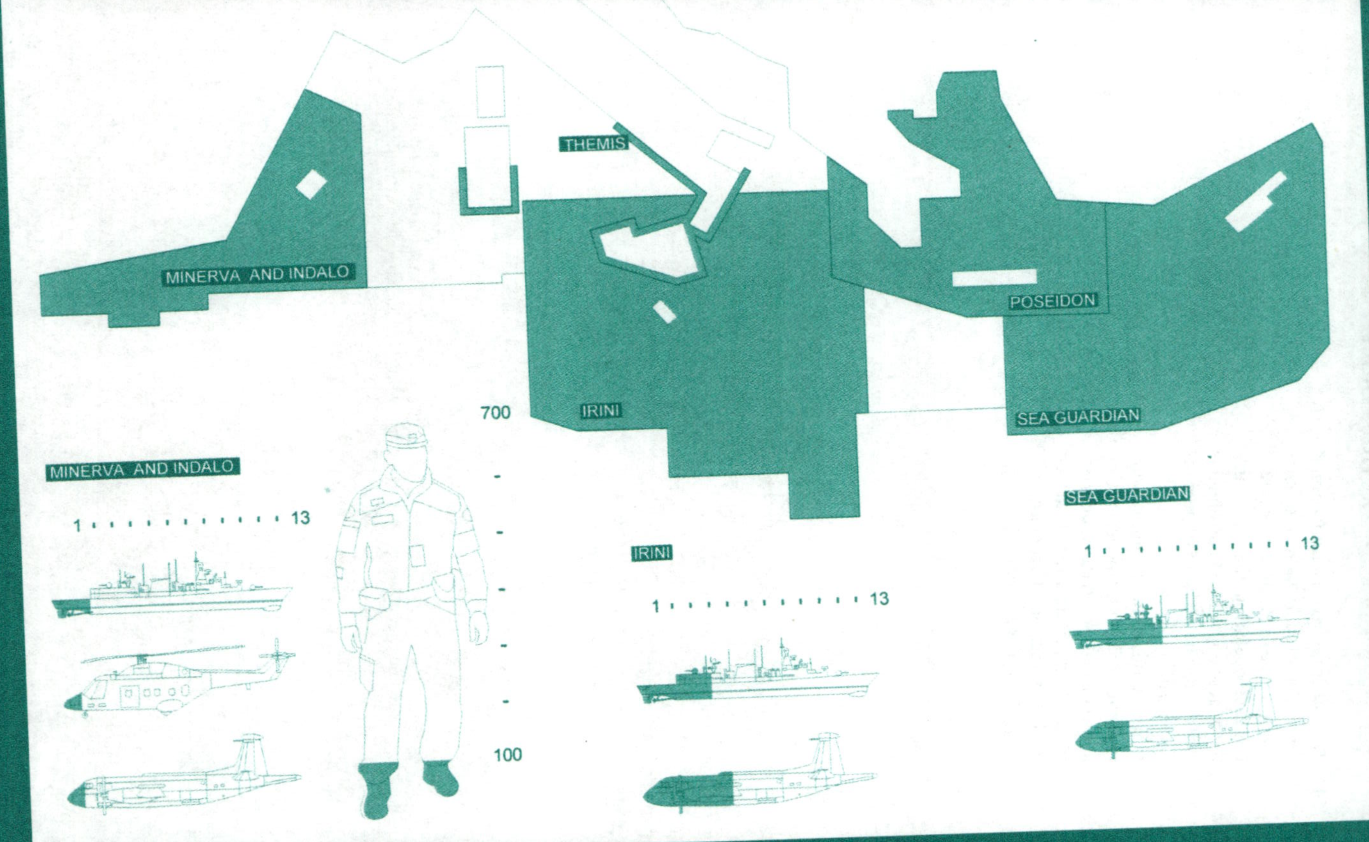

THEMIS
MINERVA AND INDALO
POSEIDON
IRINI
SEA GUARDIAN
700
100
MINERVA AND INDALO
1 13
IRINI
1 13
SEA GUARDIAN
1 13

54 *The military assets and armed forces deployed in operations currently active in the Mediterranean.* For each operation, the total number of active assets and personnel is indicated. The division of personnel into different tasks is not taken into account, including border surveillance officers, fingerprinting and registration officers, debriefing and screening experts, stolen vehicle detection officers and advanced level document officers.

Immune Mythologies: The Virus as Shaper of Social Space

Chiara Davino, Lorenza Villani

The novel coronavirus infects human bodies and, through the heterogeneous ways in which it materializes, inscribes itself into social bodies, remarking the value of the body not only as a biological given, but also as an inscription field of socio-cultural codes, highlighting the simultaneously natural and cultural character of the whole human species.[1]

A similar and hybrid interpretation can be adopted for the virus itself, referring to the concept of *quasi-object* coined by Michel Serres and successively taken up by Bruno Latour: an entity specifically non-human and natural/cultural, produced as much by the environment as by society. This interpretation, which sees the virus as a node in an uninterrupted chain of several different (natural/cultural) factors both spatially and chronologically far apart, is in contrast with the entirely different visualization of the virus as a mythology. This negates the hybrid and tentacular nature of the virus and isolates it in the mere natural dimension, to be read as an enemy and use it as projection of everything that is considered ab-normal,

58

1   Instead of the deeply rooted neocolonialist tendency to emphasize the natural character of the population of the south of the world, compared to the West, according to a different interpretation of calamities and epidemics when they hit the two different hemispheres: part of a natural cycle in the former, exceptional historical events of a transformative nature in the latter.

a-political, anti-social. This visualization favors the construction of *immune mythologies* that define Western contemporary society as a product of a systemic immune mechanism.[2]

The two different ways to see or understand the COVID-19 virus, as a natural/cultural product or as a mythology, highlight the different socio-ecological and spatial possibilities which the SARS-CoV-2 pandemic opens. On one side, forms of cohabitation between species—besides the limited concept of *urban*, still strongly tied to the space of the traditional Western city—and in favor of an awareness of the interweaving of environment, human beings, pathogens or non-human species, which overturns the relations of possession and dependency that characterized the relationship between humans and nature until now. On the other, increasingly drastic forms of social atomization, blind to any reinterpretation of our condition as a species and particularly focused on the internal oppositions within the human race itself.

Putting a particular emphasis on the immune mythopoetic mechanisms which arise from the interpretation of the virus

2   See Roberto Esposito, *Immunitas. Protezione e negazione della vita* (Torino: Einaudi, 2002).

as a *modern myth*, quoting Ernst Cassirer,[3] or *technicized myth*, according to Károly Kerényi,[4] serves the purpose of exposing the instrumentalized image which the virus took on for specific political-securitarian ends on an urban and territorial level.

QUASI-OBJECT AND HYPER-OBJECT

The first meaning, which reads the virus as a *quasi-object*, allows for an overcoming of the oppositional distinction between human and non-human entities, respectively and traditionally intended as active subjects and passive objects, in favor of a vision which interprets the latter as true social actors which invert the usual relationships. Referring to the *parasite*, Serres defines the quasi-object as an entity that cannot be a *subject*, as it is not an individual, but cannot be an *object* either, because it is an elemental builder of relations and intersubjectivity. The parasite, intended as a quasi-object, is the *primordial relation* at the root of every

60

3   As opposed to the *ancient myth*. See Ernst Cassirer, *The myth of the state* (New Haven: Yale University Press, 1946).

4   The opposition by Kerényi is towards the *genuine myth* and thus argued in Furio Jesi, *Mito* (Milano: Isedi, 1973), 107.

relationship.[5] To further articulate this assumption, Serres resorts to the metaphor of the hot potato game: the potato—metaphor for the quasi-object and thus the parasite—defines a network by going from hand to hand, it defines an *us*, which is the result of the exchange and continuous and reciprocal substitution of the *self* starting from the object-potato, which indicates subjectivity and each time establishes unexpected relationships between the players.[6] We *parasitize* each other, as much in reproduction as in social organization, thus creating ever-changing relationships which don't define the *us* as a sum of *selves*, but as a step of the *Self-in-relationship*. Particularly, the quasi-objects intended as vectors, continuously articulate phenomena on different scales which change the relation between object and subject—for example, the object-globe which, in the anthropocene, becomes *subject* reacting to our actions and making us dependent on objects and effects which depend on us.

The quasi-objects, defined as *hairy* by Latour in opposition to the *bald* ones

---

5   Michel Serres, *The Parasite* (Baltimore: John Hopkins University Press, 1982, reprint, Minneapolis: University of Minnesota Press, 2007), 225–227.
6   Ibid.

devoid of risks and uncertainties, therefore do not exist in opposition to the subject, but co-exist with it, both intended as links of the same natural/cultural chain. Hairy objects are assemblers of nature and society together, builders of collective realities: they bind scientific objectivity, which makes them readable, to more or less unforeseen socio-spatial consequences, which manifest themselves in deep temporalities, and to the symbolic and moral projections which follow.[7] The hole in the Ozone layer, AIDS, GMOs and the novel coronavirus can be interpreted as such.

The networks woven by the hairy objects, intended by Donna Haraway with a distinctly purposeful meaning as *kinships* between human and non-human *companion species*, are always *infective*, thus transformative, and bringers of mutual responsibilities.[8] To generate kinships is an exercise of forms of responsibility but also of care; the quasi-objects, or hyper-objects according to Timothy Morton, impose on the human the care of the non-human when the latter

---

7   Bruno Latour, "Note sur certains objets chevelus," *Nouvelle Revue d'Ethnopsychiatrie*, no. 27 (1994): 21–36.

8   Donna Haraway, *Chthulucene. Sopravvivere su un pianeta infetto*, trans. Claudia Durastanti and Clara Ciccioni (Roma: Nero, 2019), 14–15. Original edition: *Staying with the Trouble – Making Kin in the Chthulucene* (Chicago: University of Chicago Press, 2016).

makes contact with the former, through the assumption of an ethic of otherness based on closeness with what is *other* from us.[9]

Hyper-objects, entities widely distributed within time and space, and non-local despite their manifestations being just that, exist on different temporal scales compared to those we are used to, and show their effects in an inter-objective way:[10] when the human comes into contact with the non-human, a stance is imposed on the former towards the latter, of a trans-dimensional type. Indeed, exactly as is happening with the novel coronavirus, we are facing a quasi-object which crosses at the same time biological organisms and global social networks, a hyper-object with temporally situated local manifestations which, albeit re-articulating in the immediate perception the relationship between present and future, flattening it into an eternal present, reflects and shows relationships of cause and effect that are both wide and widely extended over both space and time.[11]

63

---

9   Timothy Morton, *Iperoggetti. Filosofia ed ecologia dopo la fine del mondo*, trans. Vincenzo Santarcangelo (Roma: Nero, 2018), 161. Original edition: *Hyperobjects* (Minneapolis: University of Minnesota Press, 2013).

10 Timothy Morton, *The Ecological Thought* (Cambridge: Harvard University Press, 2010), 130–135.

11 One need only think about the fact that human pressure on the natural environment favored and continues to favor processes of zoonosis, the passage of microorganisms, parasites or fungi from animals to humans, as was proven in the cases of SARS-CoV and MERS-CoV, respectively jumped from masked palm civets (*Paguma larvata*) and dromedaries (*Camelus dromedarius*) to humans.

MYTHOLOGICAL MACHINE
AND RISK

To this modality of visualization, that of the virus as mythology is opposed; while the former attaches an agency to the non-human similar to that of humans, the latter is strongly anthropocentric and confers to everything that is different from it an instrumental and passive character. The virus as mythology is a dispositif which shapes the social space in depth, far beyond the current spatial classifications, on a national scale, in chromatic zones that transcend the high, medium and moderate risk.[12]

Going back to the mechanism of mythological machine conceptualized by Furio Jesi,[13] the virus as a mythology consolidates the socio-spatial immune mythologies dating from before the appearance of the virus itself, and articulates new ones within the contemporary pandemic scenario, through recurring patterns which

64

---

12   The definition of *red zone*, first introduced in the Italian common language in June 2001 for the Genoa G8, has been consolidated in the common use on February 23, 2020 with a decree by the Italian Health Ministry, together with the President of the Regione Lombardia, which established the lockdown of the town of Codogno, location of the first outbreak of SARS-CoV-2 in the country. Later, several presidential decrees have classified and divided the Italian national territory in further red, orange, yellow and white zones, all of which are related to a various degrees of risk of infection.

13   See Furio Jesi, "La festa e la macchina mitologica," *Materiali Mitologici* (Torino: Einaudi, 1976): 81–120.

operate on spaces, uses and languages. Such mythologies, always empirically verifiable as preventive, securitarian, exclusive and atomizing social relationships, and thus read as the only possible categories to eradicate the virus, consolidate social juxtapositions. This mechanism, as will be shown later, is particularly fruitful in function of the joint operativity which ties, other than the conceptual analogy, the *myth* to the *risk*.

Reading the virus as a mythology is equal to seeing it as a rhetorical product, semiotic and communicative of the power mechanism of the mythological machine. The mythological machine is a conceptual space which hides within an extra-historical content, the myth, continuously referenced by its verifiable and tangible products, the mythologies. By instrumentalizing the mythical object for political ends and thus making it *technicized*, the machine mobilizes the masses through thematic repertoires and recurring narrative structures.[14] The technicized myth, as opposed to the ancient and genuine one, which stems from the collective human conscience and is a perfect fusion with the divine,[15] enjoys a particular aura among the masses and for this very reason is used and

14 Ibid.
15 See Cassirer, *The myth of the state* ; See Jesi, *Mito*.

manipulated by the authorities and those who hold the power to operate the machine to orient these towards a specific direction.[16] The mythological machine can be seen as a dispositif with precise strategic functions, resulting from the "intersection of power relations and knowledge relations"[17] as it produces knowledge under the guise of indisputable realities which shape life—works, texts, norms, images, places, social and communicative practices.[18] It is, together with the mythologies it produces, "object of, and way to obtain, knowledge."[19]

Another knot that ties the relationship between power and knowledge to shape contemporary society in depth, through the use of projected images, is the concept of risk. According to Ulrich Beck, risks are produced only in terms of a *knowledge* which, shaping and modifying them time and time again, makes them "unknown and unwanted forces which take on the role of a dominant force within history and socie-

66

16   Jesi analyzes the manipulations of the myth and the mythological materials particularly within the scope of traditional right-wing culture through distortions of the spirit and the ancient Roman world in the key of Fascism. See Furio Jesi, *Cultura di destra* (Milano: Garzanti, 1976).
17   Giorgio Agamben, *Che cos'è un dispositivo* (Milano: Nottetempo, 2006), 7.
18   See Enrico Manera, "Furio Jesi. Un ritratto," *Giornale di filosofia della religione*, no. 6 (2015).
19   Furio Jesi, *Materiali mitologici. Mito e antropologia nella cultura mitteleuropea* (Torino: Einaudi, 2001), 339.

ty."[20] Consequently, within the *risk society*, the political and social meaning of the knowledge grows, and consequently, so does the power of those who hold the *risk knowledge* (science, politics) and have the power to spread it (mass media).[21] Within the risk society, *reflective* as it is a producer of its own risks, a risk becoming a reality is directly correlated to its media coverage; to consider a risk an ever new reality equates to continuously modifying the structure of politics, collective and individual life.

Similarly to the technicized myth, which is never separate from power but instead is codified by it, so is the risk a rhetorical, semiotic and communicative product of precise power mechanisms. Moreover, whether it is risk or myth, in both cases there is a disconnect between real events and the *images* of such events produced by mythopoetic mechanisms and predictions; both cannot be in fact understood outside of their materializations within specific mediation—whether scientific, political, economical or popular.

Mythologies and risks spread a collective knowledge of a systemic type which, based

20   Ulrich Beck, *La società del rischio. Verso una seconda modernità*, trans. Walter Privitera, Carlo Sandrelli, and Melania Mascarino (Roma: Carocci, 2000), 29. Original edition: *Risikogesellschaft. Auf dem Weg in eine andere Moderne* (Frankfurt am Main: Suhrkamp Verlag, 1986).

21   Ibid., 61.

on biased or probabilistic projections, acts in everyone and through everyone, incessantly consolidating them. Immune mythologies produced by the mythological machine within the contemporary pandemic context further structure the risk society in which the state of emergency is the rule, and fear and security project onto each other. Indeed every level of security is defined through its inverse reproduction and every subject within this society constitutes itself as a political member through the projection of an external subject deemed dangerous and non-political.[22] The logic of "worst-case scenarios," through which the risk materializes, forces a choice between which form of knowledge deserves the most credibility and consequently the rhetorical-mythopoetic strategies become decisive as a function of their ability to convince the masses.

IMMUNE MYTHOLOGIES

To argue the *systemic* operativity reached today by the immune mythopoeia within the risk society, it is essential to go back to the moment in which, in the eighteenth century, medicine went beyond the purely

22 See Andrea Cavalletti, *La città biopolitica. Mitologie della sicurezza* (Milano: Mondadori, 2005).

therapeutic action range and entered fields historically not considered strictly of a medical nature.[23]

Medicalization as a new model of power, space and work management, establishes the transition of the social body from mere statutory-political metaphor (as called by Hobbes within the *Leviathan*) to an effective biological reality and medical field of action.[24] Michel Foucault conceptualizes such transition resorting to the idea of *population*: a collective place in which the intervention of the new bio-political power is concentrated, and includes within itself not just the biological concept of species, but also that of *audience*, intended as *grabbing surface* which the species offers to be oriented in a precise direction.[25] In the *noso-politics* of the eighteenth century, public health is the hinge of the osmosis between biological, judicial and political fields, non-medical problems begin to be defined in terms of illness or disorder, and medical and social surveillance zones take shape, becoming de-socializing for life

23   See Mario Colucci, "Medicalizzazione," *JCOM Journal of Science Communication* 5, no. 1 (Trieste, 2006).
24   See Michel Foucault, "L'evoluzione della nozione di 'individuo pericoloso' nella psichiatria legale del XIX secolo," *Aut Aut*, no. 370 (2016): 125–146. Original edition: "About the concept of the 'dangerous individual' in 19th century legal psychiatry," *Journal of law and psychiatry*, no. 1 (1978).
25   Michel Foucault, *Sécurité, territoire, population. Cours au Collège de France (1977-1978)* (Paris: Gallimard Seuil, 2004), 77.

but able to make it immune from any kind of communal drift according to health and general public safety. The following correspondence between measures of a sanitary nature and measures of socio-economic exclusion, began between the eighteenth and nineteenth centuries,[26] has today been consolidated and has evolved in more sophisticated and general practices of *immunization* which bend a biological function into an instrument through which it is possible to manage the widespread defensive need towards everything that is considered *foreign*.

Immunity, the *securitarian* answer to a risk, is the "mythical iconic object"[27] which shaped modern society and continues to shape the contemporary one precisely because in it risk and security operate in depth—one need only to think about the post-2001 securitarian policies which proliferated globally to contrast the terrorist threat, and their subsequent generalization to face yet another *other*, each time different.

In 2020 this otherness manifested globally as a virus which, ontologically micro-

70

---

26 For example, the separation between rich and poor working-class neighborhoods put in effect in England throughout the nineteenth century is a consequence of the Cholera epidemic of 1832 in the United Kingdom.
27 Donna Haraway, *Manifesto Cyborg. Donne, tecnologie e biopolitiche del corpo*, trans. Liana Borghi (Milano: Feltrinelli, 1995), 137. Original edition: *A Cyborg Manifesto* (New York: Routledge, 1991).

scopic and invisible, has sharpened the collective exophobia well beyond the viral agent. Immunity intended as inclusion of what one wants excluded in a form that makes its pathogenic consequences tolerable, becomes through the mythological machine's mechanisms, *immune mythology* based on an ontological and insurmountable incompatibility between the self and the other. The rhetorically decisive transition performed by the machine which deforms the idea of immunity by turning it into a *technicized myth*, is its aggressive military formulation. When

> the immune mechanism takes on the shape of a proper war for the control and, ultimately, the survival of the body against foreign invaders who want to occupy it first and then destroy it[28]

the annihilation of the *enemy* at any cost is required. Analyzing the formulation in military terms of the immune process, Roberto Esposito also highlights how there is a mythical idea in this reconstruction, which negates any kind of vulnerability by the invaded subject[29]—a particularly recur-

---

28   See Esposito, *Immunitas*, 149–150.
29   Ibid., 155–156.

ring rhetorical element within the (institutional) narrative formulas of the mythological machine.

The mythopoetic processes in place within the contemporary pandemic context, operating on the population as much as a species as an audience, manifest themselves by way of languages and narrations, spaces, uses and practices, laws; but also through profound effects on mental health, behavioral disorders and moods, making the viral infection also a, deeply, *psycho-social* one.[30]

The warlike language which permeates the immune mythopoetic communication, even beyond the pandemic context, allows for the institutions to justify not only the exceptionality of the initiatives and measures taken—nothing can be considered excessive during a pure emergency—but even the loss of human lives inasmuch as inevitable consequence of a conflict. It is within this framing operation that the glorification of the army of angels and martyrs—doctors and other medical personnel—

72

---

30 While the incidence of health disorders on mental health is frequent in pandemic contexts in general (recently the SARS epidemic of 2003 and the Ebola epidemic of 2014) and with long-lasting effects, the contemporary pandemic cannot be compared to the previous ones because of its homogenous spread on a global scale and the lengthy domestic lockdown, and so are its effects. See Maria Rosa Gualano et al., "Effects of COVID-19 Lockdown on Mental Health and Sleep Disturbances in Italy," *International Journal of Environmental Research and Public Health* (July 2, 2020).

because of their unavoidable sacrifice, takes place, and so does the frequent use of the expression "losing people before their time," which inevitably refers to the sacrifice of human lived which the condition of war requires.[31] To be part of a military frame allows, moreover, to discontinue the normal temporal dimension and be established into that of waiting, in which every real decision is postponed, and every contingent fact, understood as urgent sense of danger, requires an immediate mobilization—an aspect particularly evident in *the war on SARS-CoV-2* since, as Jesi argues, "every true change in the experience of time is a ritual that requires a human sacrifice."[32]

Resorting to the consolidation of the much easier visualization of the virus as *enemy to be destroyed*, rather as natural/cultural entity come in contact with the human species as a consequence of anthropic processes towards the environment, the immune mythologies de-humanize as much those who find themselves beyond the frontlines (the national borders) because potential

---

31 The building of the *imagined community* of the nation is based on the sacrifice of life and the *compensatory immortality*. See Zygmunt Bauman, *Paura liquida*, trans. Marco Cupellaro (Roma-Bari: Laterza, 2009), 48–49. Original edition: *Liquid fear* (Cambridge: Policy Press, 2006).

32 Furio Jesi, *Spartakus. Simbologia della rivolta* (Torino: Bollati Boringhieri, 2000), 31.

vector of an illness that always comes from the outside, as the majority of the *casualties*, unavoidable losses in war. They make the masses compliant towards whatever authoritarian drift, and even spark in them a spasmodic need for norms, rules, predictability, uniformity, of stigmatization and accusation of deviant behavior within a low-intensity conflict in which every individual feels like an active element of the war landscape.[33]

Beyond the establishment of *red zones* and introduction of tracking systems—which constitute the spatial effect of a similar process of translation of *civilian* issues into *military* ones[34]—the iconic space of this Pandemic is the physical distancing, the meter of distance to be compulsorily kept from the other, and the gathering, understood as aggregative, chaotic and unforeseen spatiality of bodies in which the virus has found, through the recently constructed imagery, the main form of visualization.

33 An example among many is represented by the SUS (Sistema Unico di Segnalazione) digital platform in which, during the first Italian national lockdown, the citizens of Rome could report any public gathering observed in the streets from the windows of their own home to the authorities.
34 In Italy the app Immuni was launched in June 2020 by the Presidency of the Council of Ministers in collaboration with the Health Ministry and the Ministry for Technological Innovation and Digitalization. Tracking systems, both institutional or not, which outline diversified scenarios of conflict between individual privacy and collective security have nonetheless been introduced on a global scale to help contain the Pandemic.

TO BE SUBJECTED TO CATASTROPHIC
AND THREATENING PREDICTIONS OF THE
FUTURE, AND A MEDIA BOMBARDMENT
BY THE DAILY BULLETIN CENTERED ON
THE INCREASING NUMBER OF DEATHS,
INFECTIONS, OVERCROWDED INTENSIVE
CARE UNITS IN HOSPITALS UNABLE TO
ACCOMODATE MORE SICK PEOPLE,
CAN COMPROMISE RELATIONSHIPS,
SOCIABILITY AND ANY IMMEDIATE AND
FUTURE PLANNING IN ADOLESCENTS
(A DEVELOPMENTAL STAGE IN
WHICH EMOTIONS, COGNITIONS AND
RELATIONSHIPS ARE ORIENTED TOWARDS
A POSITIVE FUTURE OF EXPANDING
EXPECTATIONS AND OPPORTUNITIES).
ACCORDING TO A STUDY CONDUCTED IN
ITALY AND ONLINE BY THE UNIVERSITY
OF CATANIA BETWEEN APRIL 15 AND
MAY 15, 2020 ON A SAMPLE OF 148
STUDENTS AGED BETWEEN 17 AND 19,
THE PANDEMIC CAN WORSEN EXISTING
MENTAL HEALTH PROBLEMS, AND LEAD
TO MORE AND NEW CASES AMONG
CHILDREN AND ADOLESCENTS. THE
CONTEMPORARY SOMATIZATION OF A
NEBULOUS, CONFUSED, UNCERTAIN AND
DISTRESSING FUTURE IS MOSTLY RELATED
TO BREATHING DIFFICULTIES.

See Pietro Smirni, Gioacchino Lavanco, and Daniela Smirni, "Anxiety in Older Adolescents at the Time of COVID-19," *Journal of Clinical Medicine* (September 23, 2020).

The premises by Bryan Turner according to which illness is a form of language, the body a representation and medicine a political practice,[35] consolidate the argument that sees immune mythologies take on the atomization of the gathered bodies, by virtue of a viral representation, as a practice first and foremost of a *medical* nature—and clearly political. The medical and political control bodies, gestures and bodily performances of apparition is the mechanism that is bringing the confusion, even on different fields such as that of common language, the radically different expressions of *social distancing* and *physical distancing*—today used as synonyms.

The contemporary social space, sequence of securitized enclaves on different scales and instituted to face continuous states of crisis, is today further fragmented in a hierarchical succession of collective spatial realities, made possible or forbidden according to the degree of danger attributed to them, and associated to the possible happening of gatherings.[36] Space goes from being a place for plural apparition exercises to

35 Bryan S. Turner, *The Body and Society* (New York: Blackwell, 1984), 177.
36 The presidential decree (DPCM) of October 24, 2020 establishes, for example, the closure of every theater, concert hall, cinema and other open-air spaces used for representations and shows. On the contrary, it allows limited access to places of worship, while taking into consideration the places' size and characteristics.

mere geometry, *measurable* in some cases and often *unknowable*, in which to exercise only those activities that are considered essential. The restriction imposed on every social relationship that is *not essential* consolidates, therefore, the process as a whole. The epidemic is not then simply used as a metaphor for the social disorder and everything that is frowned upon, but *is* the totality of the social body itself and its unforeseen gatherings. The only square meters exempt from this logic are those of homes, framed by the mythopoetic mechanisms in the candid frame of a *refuge*. The forced hyper-connection of the domestic hearth, today a new spatiality of a true urban nature, is thus further consolidating the process of transformation of the domestic landscape that began in the middle of the twentieth century with the introduction of radio and television technologies.

Through the space and inside the domestic space, well before the appearance of COVID-19 and especially nowadays, there has therefore been a further step towards the transition from forms of disciplinary and architectural control to forms of micro-prosthetic and media-cybernetic control.[37]

---

37 Paul B. Preciado, "Learning from the Virus," *ArtForum* (April–May 2020).

THE PSYCHOLOGICAL CONSEQUENCES OF
QUARANTINE (FRUSTRATION, SOLITUDE,
PREOCCUPATION FOR THE FUTURE) ARE RISK
FACTORS FOR MENTAL ILLNESS SUCH AS
ANXIETY, AFFECTION DISORDERS, PSYCHOSIS.
COMPARING DATA GATHERED IN THE
NORTHERN, CENTRAL AND SOUTHERN ITALY BY
A STUDY CONDUCTED ONLINE BY THE SAPIENZA
UNIVERSITY OF ROME BETWEEN MARCH 18 AND
31, 2020 ON A SAMPLE OF 2291 RESPONDENTS
(MOSTLY WITHIN THE 18-29 YEARS RANGE)
THERE EMERGES HOW THE PSYCHOLOGICAL
STATE IS NOT INFLUENCED SOLELY BY DIRECT
FACTORS (FEAR OF CONTAGION) BUT ALSO—
AND MOSTLY—BY INDIRECT CONSEQUENCES
OF THE PANDEMIC (ISOLATION AND SOCIAL
DISTANCING MEASURES) WHICH HIT EVERY
REGION OF THE WORLD EQUALLY. WHILE
NORTHERN ITALY WAS IMPACTED MORE
SEVERELY AND WAS THE FIRST AREA TO BE
PUT IN LOCKDOWN (A CONDITION WHICH
WOULD HAVE SUGGESTED A HARDER IMPACT
ON MENTAL HEALTH COMPARED TO THE
CENTER AND SOUTH), MOOD ALTERATION
VALUES, POST-TRAUMATIC SYMPTOMS AND
ANXIETY REGISTERED WERE BARELY HIGHER
THAN THOSE REGISTERED IN THE CENTER
AND SOUTH. THE STATE OF ANXIETY, FOR
EXAMPLE, REACHED LEVELS OF 12,72%, 11,77%
AND 12,47% RESPECTIVELY FOR NORTHERN,
CENTRAL AND SOUTHERN ITALY.

See Giuseppe Forte et al., "The Enemy Which Sealed the World: Effects of COVID-19
Diffusion on the Psychological State of the Italian Population," Journal of Clinical
Medicine (June 10, 2020).

The distortion of the concept of immunity within immune mythology goes through an infodemic, a usual practice by today's society, especially when hit by a pandemic. The media coverage of the virus rules through the polarization of information on the virus and its numerous representations and personifications. The background on which this information is projected is one of *generalized* pandemic danger which leads to a danger of *extinction* heterogeneous in its facets—extinction of the species, class, ethnicity. The virus-biological-agent becomes linguistic-media-virus which, through precise practices, infects the rational reading, interpretation and human thought processes. The infodemic does not merely emerge by way of an overabundance of often inaccurate information, but also in the more sophisticated production and sharing of myths and superficial beliefs which affect the transversal and deeper readings of the processes underway. The myth of the pandemic as a great equalizer and the virus as equalizer of society's inequalities, for example, has widely spread through headline news in the first months of 2020 when the first cases of infection included people that were *also* within the elites. The differences in the access to healthcare, the residential overcrowding caused by the lock-

down, the nutritional insecurity sparked by
the halting of every type of job that could not
be performed from home, however, increase
the exposure of some social groups to the
virus, its potential mortality and its effects,
thus exposing the mythical interpretations.[38]

38 See Michael Marmot and Jessica Allen, "COVID-19: exposing and amplifying
inequalities," *J Epidemiol Community Health*, no. 74 (2020): 681–682.

THE COCOS (COVID COLLATERAL IMPACTS) INQUIRY, CONDUCTED IN ITALY AND ONLINE BY THE UNIVERSITY OF TURIN BETWEEN APRIL 19 AND MAY 3, 2020 ON A SAMPLE OF 1515 PEOPLE (MEDIAN AGE 42 YEARS), HIGHLIGHTS THAT YOUNG ADULTS ARE MORE LIKELY TO SHOW DEPRESSION (24,7%), ANXIETY (23,2%) AND SLEEP DISORDERS (42,2% OUT OF WHICH 17,4% WITH MODERATE INSOMNIA) COMPARED TO OTHER AGE RANGES BECAUSE MORE SUSCEPTIBLE TO THE INFODEMIC, WIDESPREAD OVER SOCIAL NETWORKS, AND THE SUBSEQUENT INCREASE IN RISK PERCEPTION, AND MISTRUST AND UNJUSTIFIED INTOLERANCE TOWARDS POTENTIALLY DANGEROUS CATEGORIES. THE MEDIA UNEASE CAN FAVOR REPERCUSSIONS ON MENTAL AND PHYSICAL HEALTH, IMPACTING NEGATIVELY ON THE LONG TERM PRESSURE ON HEALTHCARE SYSTEMS.

See Gualano et al., *Effects of COVID-19 Lockdown on Mental Health and Sleep Disturbances in Italy.*

Ristoratori in protest[a]
Multa di 400 euro pe[r...]

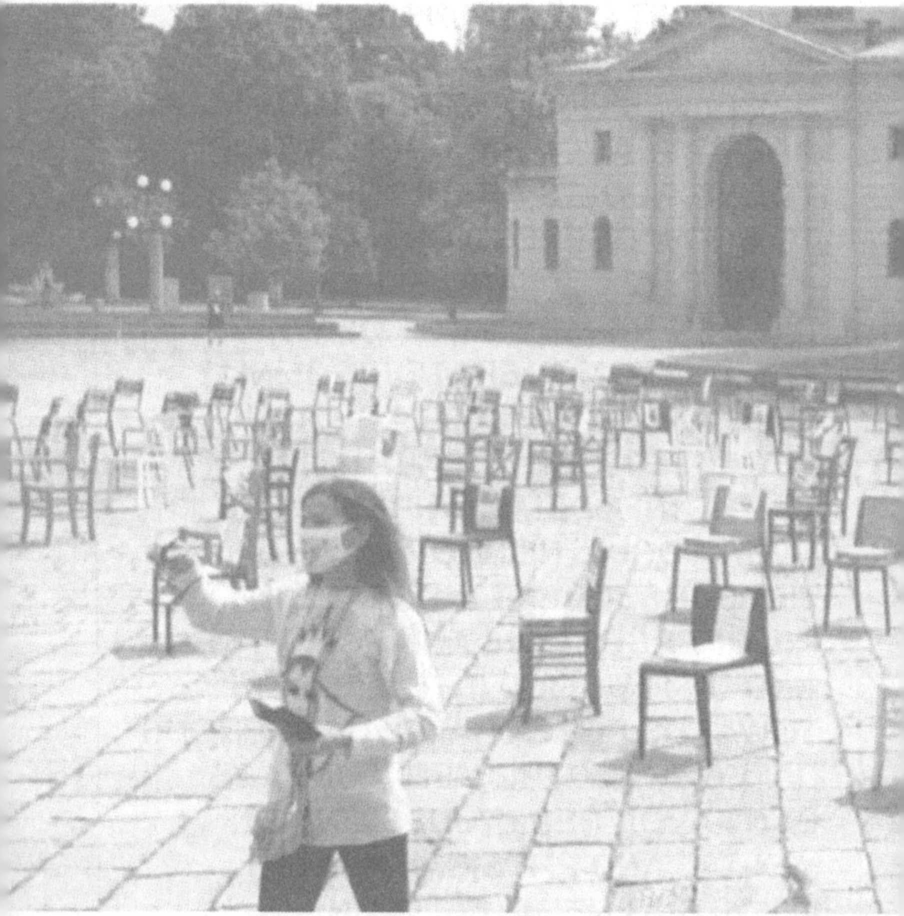

  6 Maggio 2020   Comments 0   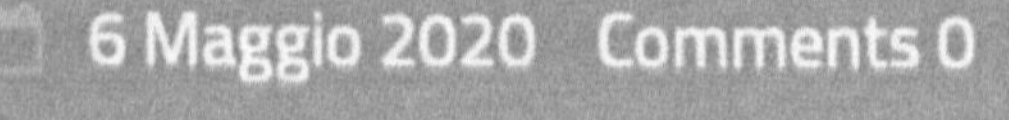 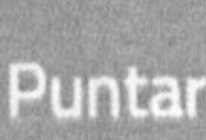 Puntare[...]

[R]istoratori in protesta multati a Milano. E' cos[ì...]
[h]anno esposto **sedie vuote sotto l'Arco della P[...]**
[s]icurezza dopo lo stop causato da una crisi se[...]

a Milano: 'Se apriam
l flash mob

cara la **manifestazione di oggi** ai ristoratori c

a Milano. Una protesta per chiedere **quando e**

recedenti nel mondo della ristorazione. Ai part

**NO alla chiusura di ristoranti e
delle palestre. NO alla chiusur
NO al Lockdown della cultura.
controlli a tappeto. Si all'apert
rispetto sempre delle norme a**

chiudere alle 18:00, dopo aver i
ingenti per la riapertura post-lo
oltre che un danno irreparabile,
camerieri, cuochi, vigilanti e qu
settore. Un danno irreparabile
l'industria della trasformazione
per palestre, operatori dello sp
teatri, cinema, sale concerto m
impiega centinaia di migliaia di
pesantissimo in questi mesi e
e rispettare le regole in manier
Rispettare con responsabilità l

ar alle 18. **NO alla chiusura
i teatri, cinema sale concerto.
alla sicurezza nei locali e ai
a in totale sicurezza e nel
covid-19.** Costringere a
estito risorse economiche
down è una vera ingiustizia
n solo per i ristoratori ma per
i lavorano a vario titolo nel
he per gli agricoltori e
roalimentare tutta. Stessa cosa
e del benessere. La chiusura di
erà in ginocchio un mondo che
iani, che ha pagato un prezzo
ha fatto di tutto per adeguarsi
ssolutamente scrupolosa.
gole ed elevare, senza sconti, i

PER CONTENERE E TRASPORTARE
MILANO. IL MOOD È MORTUARIO,
ANDREA CHERCHI CHE ACCOMPA(
ASSOMIGLIANO UN [...]

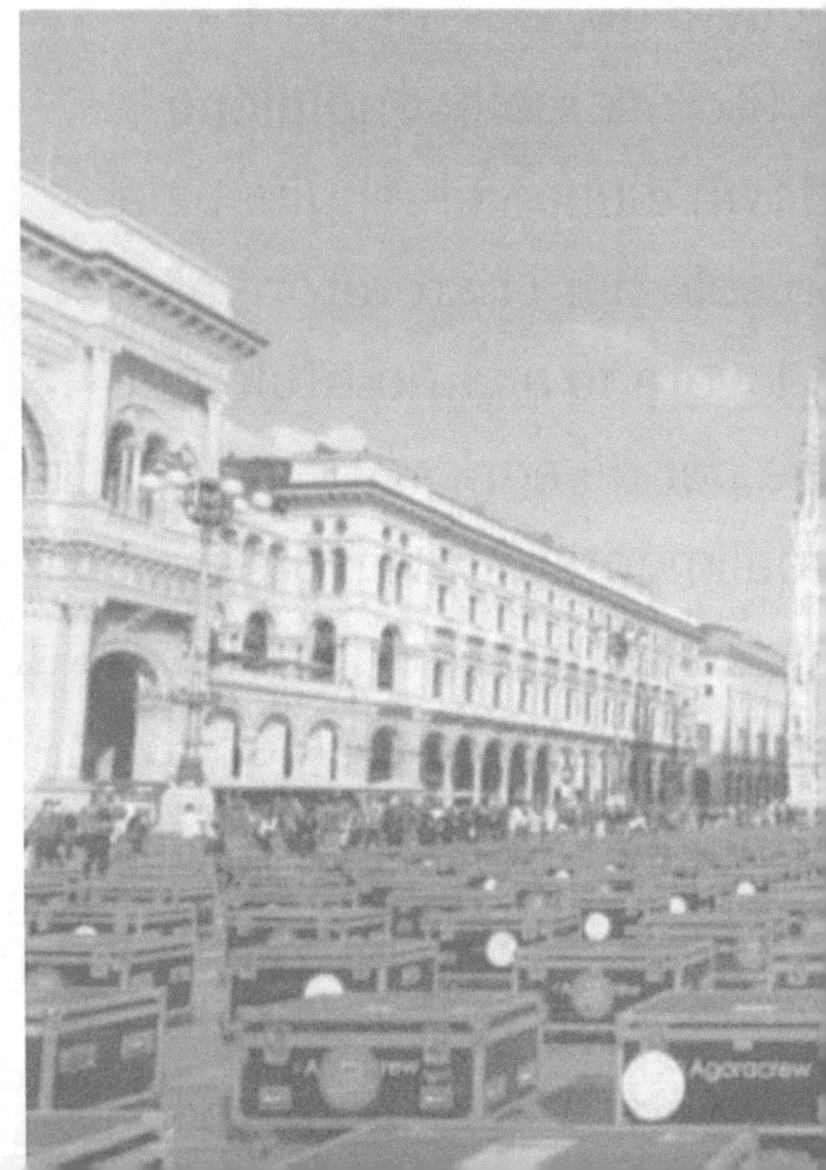

ATTREZZATURE DI SCENA, IN PIAZZA

ME DIMOSTRANO LE BELLISSIME FOT

ANO L'ARTICOLO, CON QUELLE CASSE

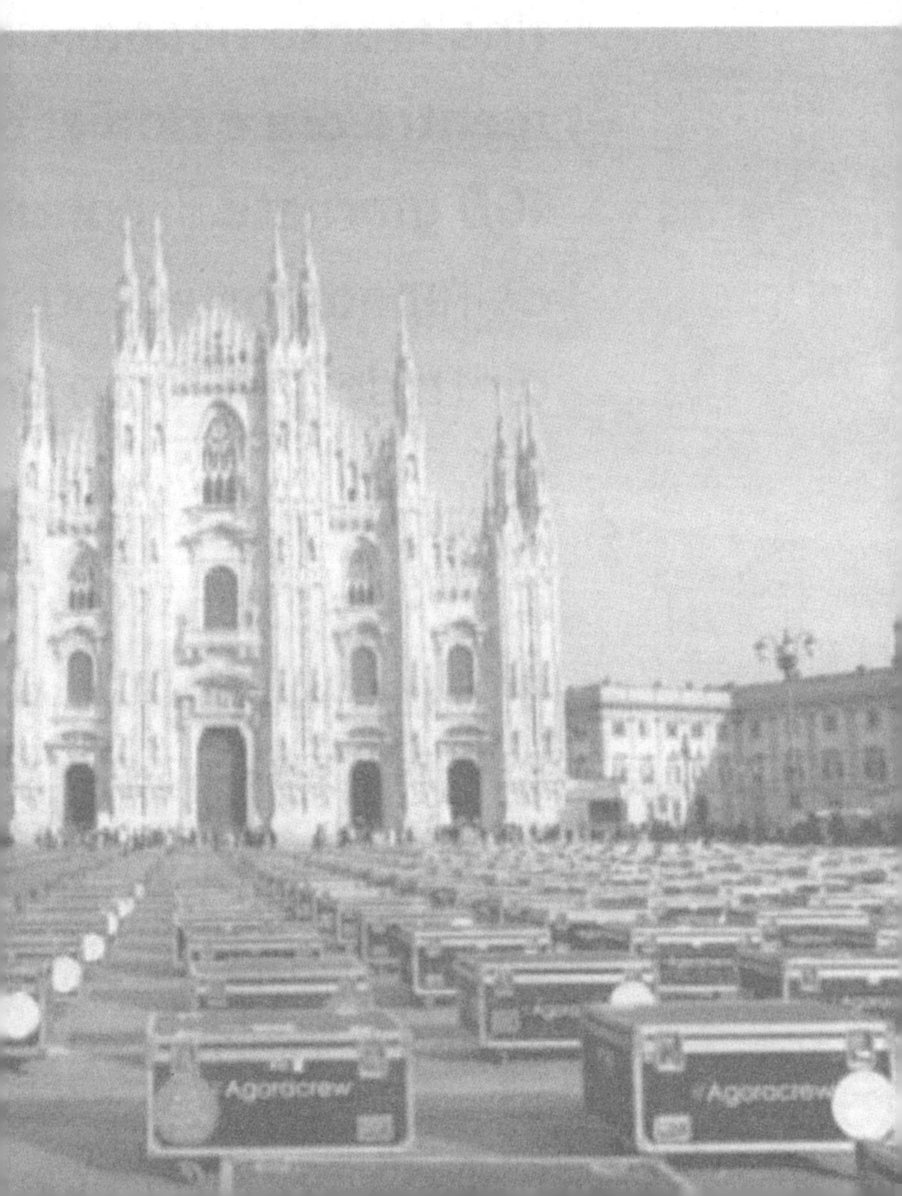

Riportiamo **di seguito le richi**
questa crisi:

1. Chiediamo che **l'inder**
    finalmente riconosci
    mentre ora è richiest
    100 giornate di contri
    dell'anno precedente:
    diritti dei lavoratori de

2. Chiediamo che l'inder
    disoccupazione Naspi
    riconosciuta agli inter
    per tutti i periodi di so
    in costanza di rapport
    almeno pari a quello l
    anche le giornate di la

3. Chiediamo per l'acce

e più urgenti per affrontare

à di malattia sia
fin dal primo giorno,
versamento minimo di
i INPS dal gennaio
ediamo semplicemente i
altri settori.

à di

tenti dello spettacolo
ensione di attività, anche
i lavoro, per un periodo
rato, considerando
o per prove.

alla Naspi, l'abolizione

Napoli, la pr[otesta dei] taxi in piazz[a del] Plebiscito: "[...] irreversibil[e il] Dpcm"

di Tiziana Cozzi

Centinaia di auto n[...]

27 OTTOBRE 2020

otesta dei

del

Danni

dal

emiciclo

d'Italia: "Morire [...] che di Covid"

Piazza del Plebiscito è stata invasa da dec[...] questi lavoratori, è rientrare tra le categor[...]

28 OTTOBRE 2020

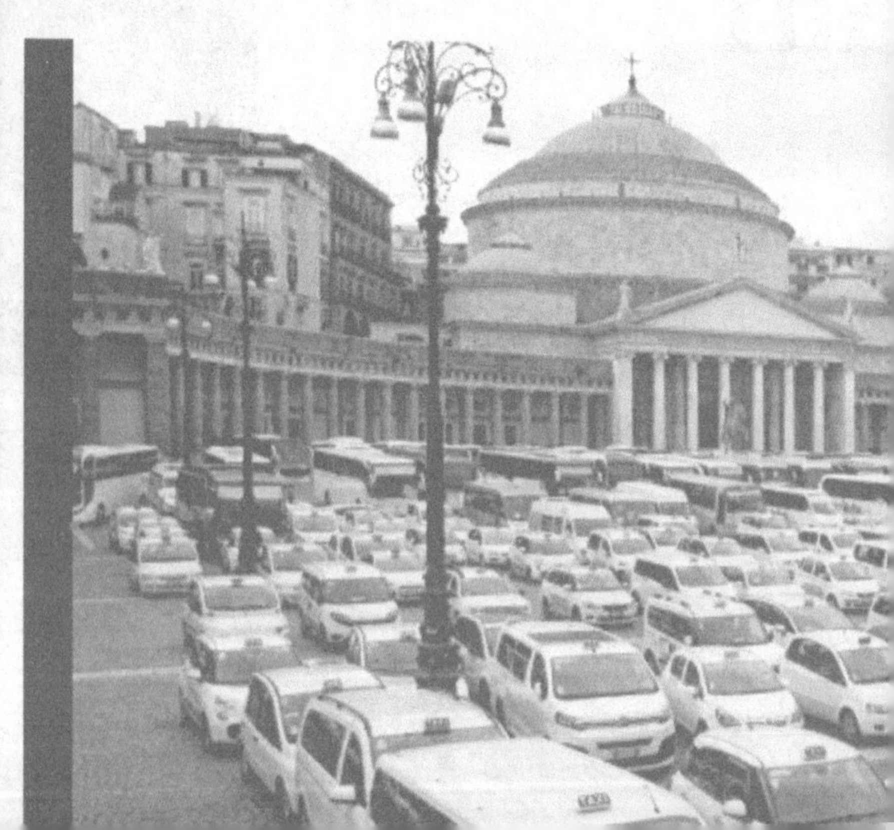

no prima di fame

i taxi, scuolabus e mezzi Ncc. La speranza, p
e saranno aiutate tramite il Decreto Ristori

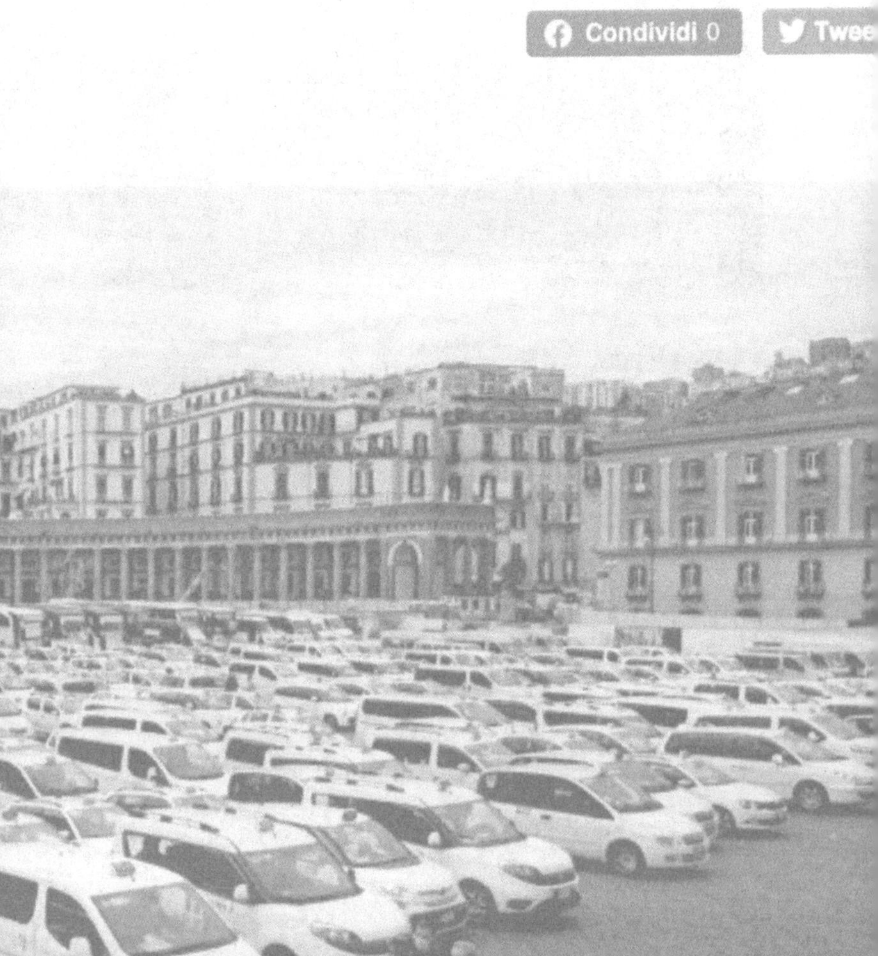

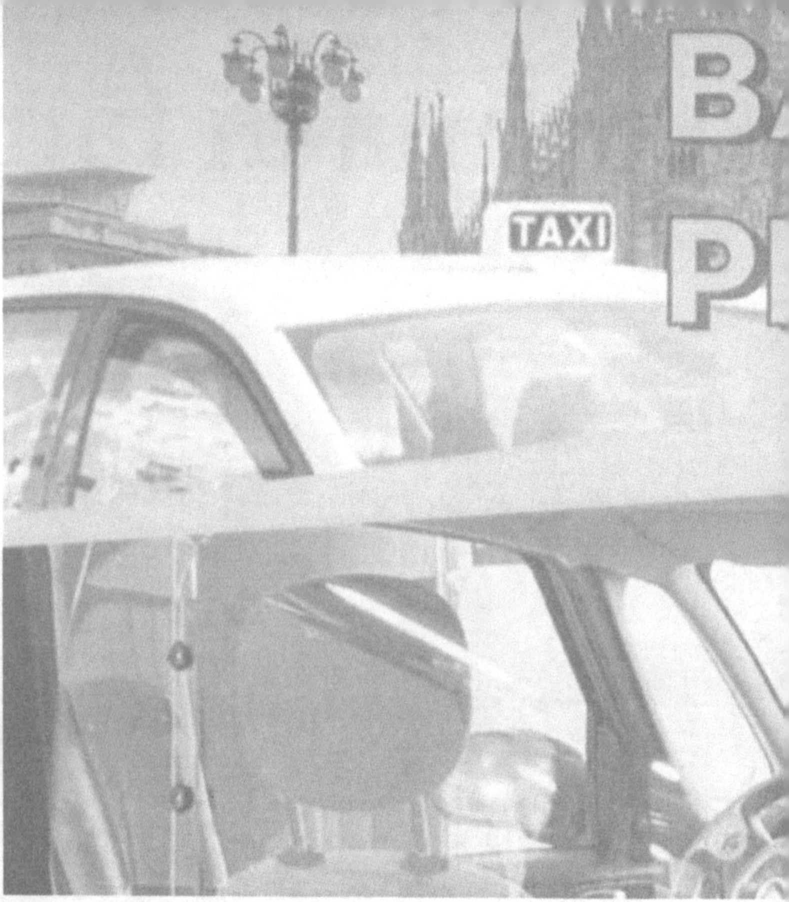

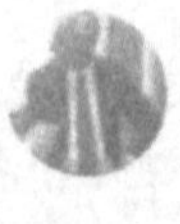

Domenico Nenna ha lanciato questa pe[...]
1 altro/altra

Per l'emergenza COVID-19, per[...]
il trasporto Taxi sia molto a RIS[...]
e degli utenti, pertanto come p[...]
batteri dico che il TAXI DEVES[...]
PERMANENTE, anche per altri[...]

RRIERA OTETTIVA

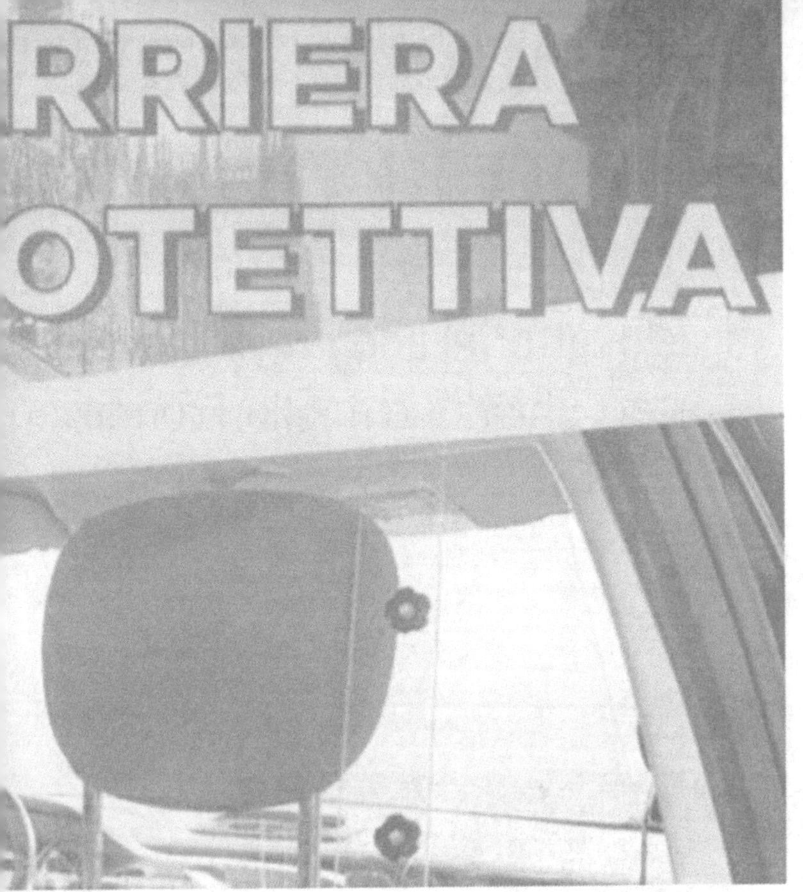

utela della salute, ritengo che
IO, per la salute dell'operatore
nziale trasportatore di virus e
E MUNITO DI DIVISORIO
di pericoli, E MAI PIÙ TOLTO

Sciopero lampo
dopo la protest

I ciclo fattorini aderenti a Glovo si s...
corteo. Chiedono migliori condizion...

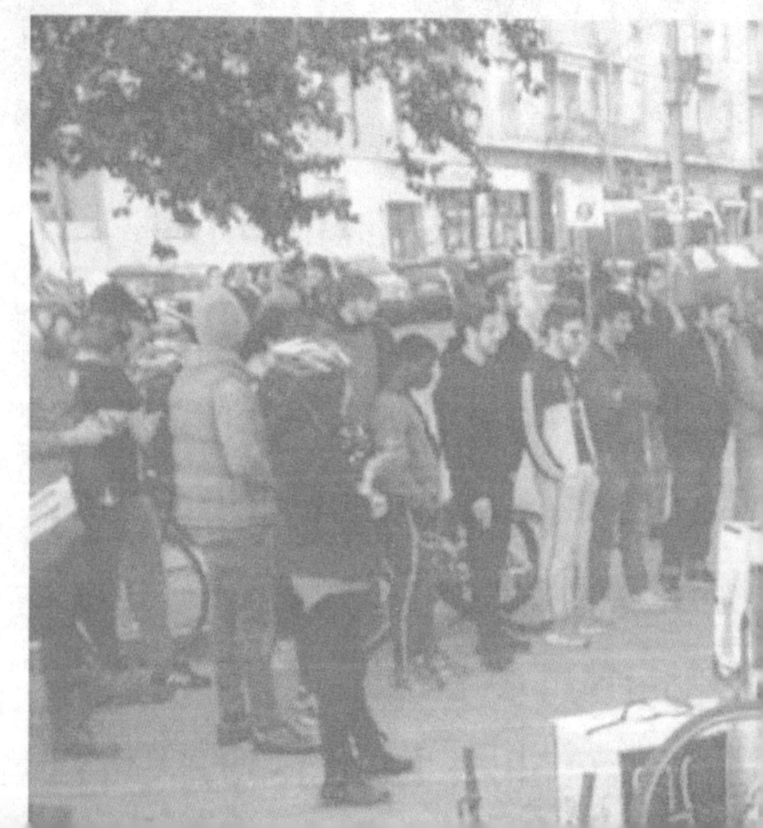

lei rider di Torino contro i clienti vip

iuniti in piazza Santa Rita e poi sono sfilati i
nomiche e di sicurezza

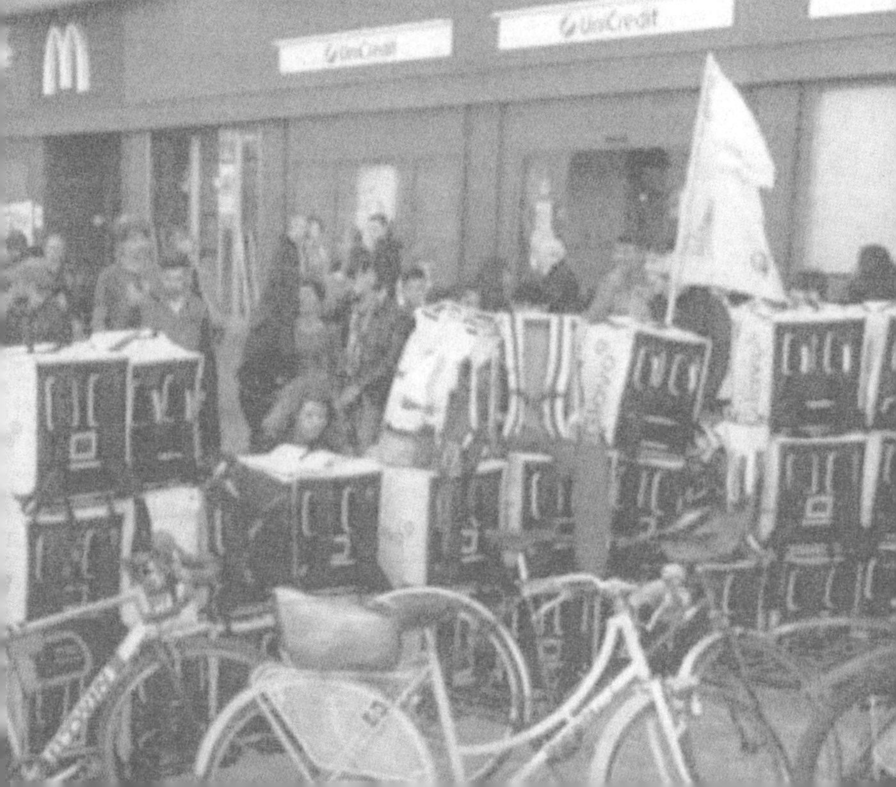

Quaranta rose b
commemorare g
Covid: il flash m

Distanziati e con indosso mascherin
silenziosamente sotto il Pirellone. L

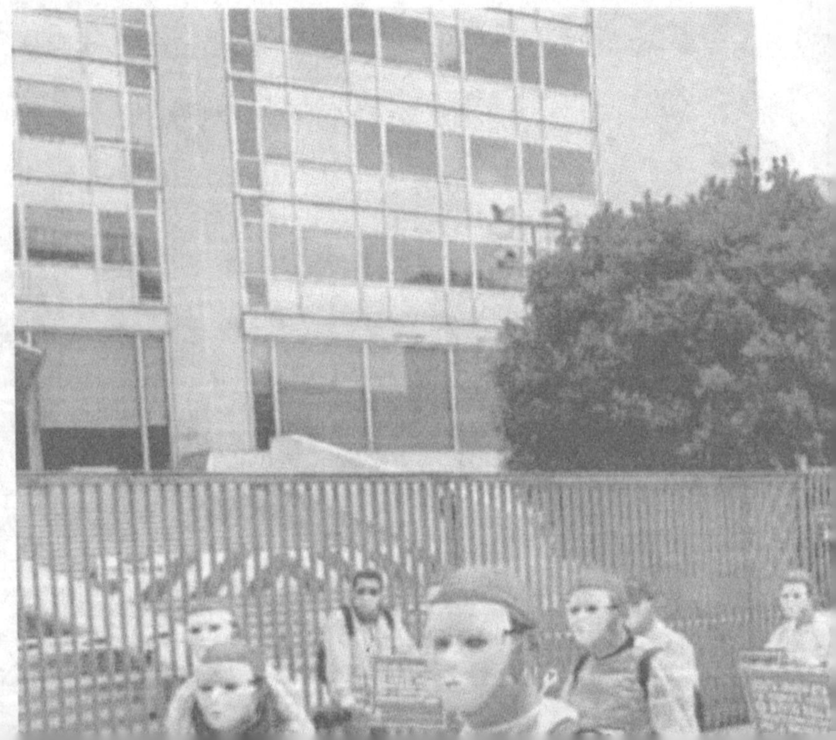

nche a terra per
infermieri morti
b in piazza

maschera bianca per protestare

anifestazione

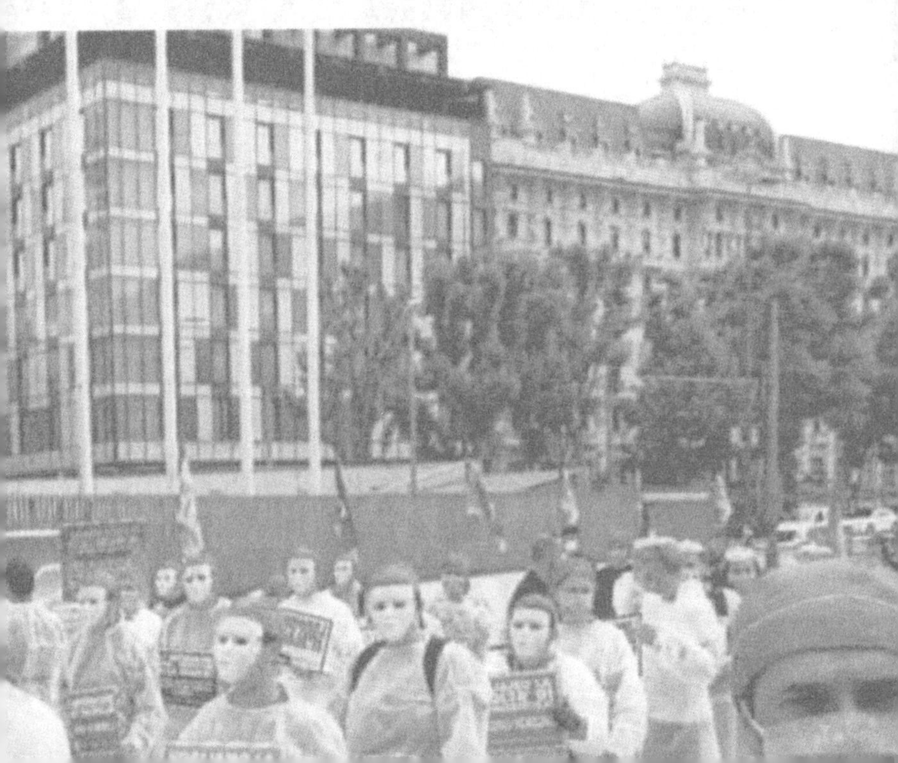

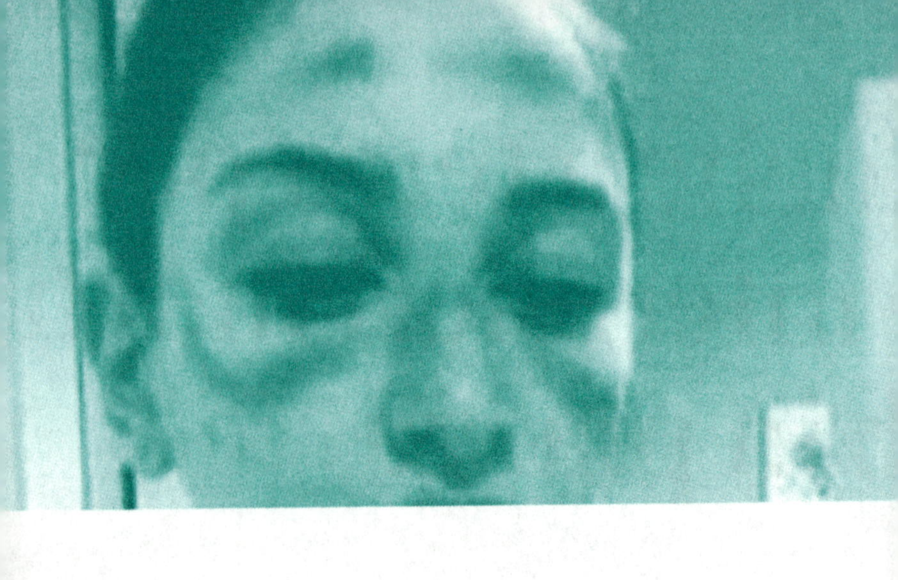

Simone Gussoni ha lancia
dell'Economia e delle Fina
li Infermieri non sta
uto, non rimandano
tanno salvando vite

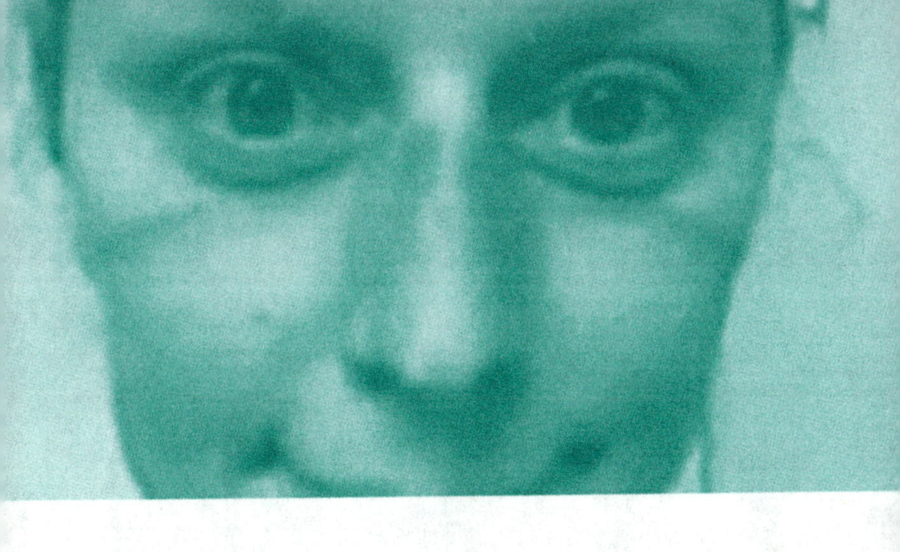

questa petizione e l'ha diretta

e) e a 5 altri/altre

no temporeggiando

lavoro a domani.

questo momento, e

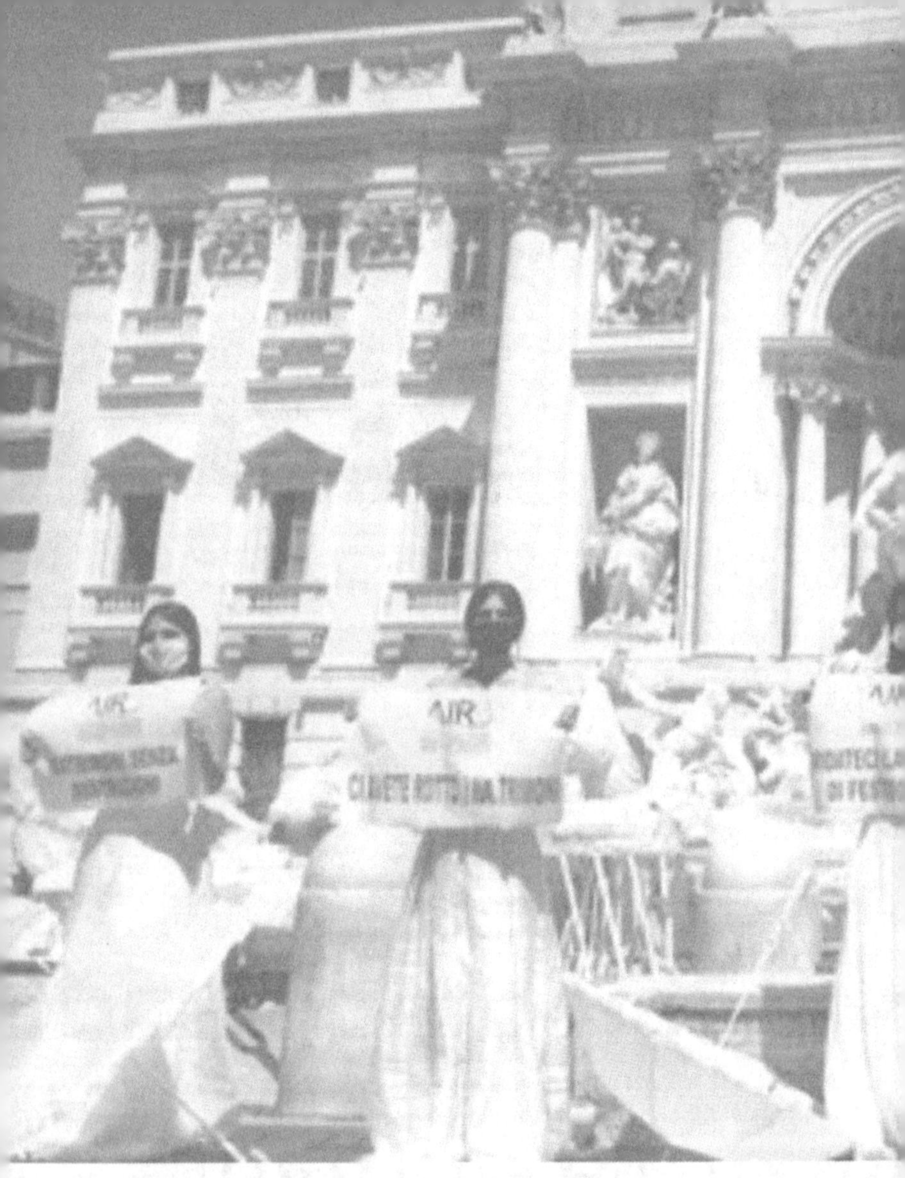

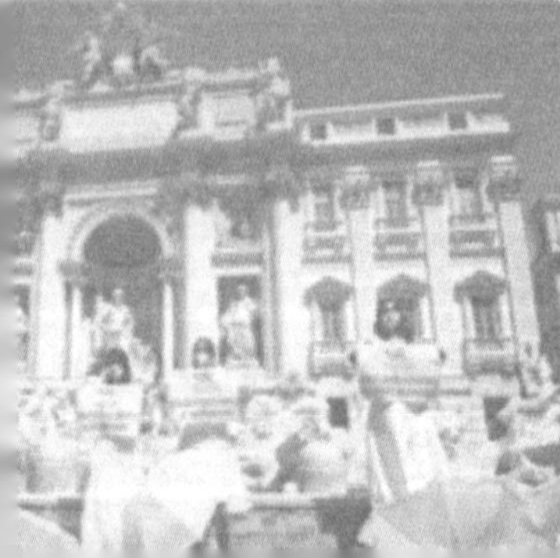
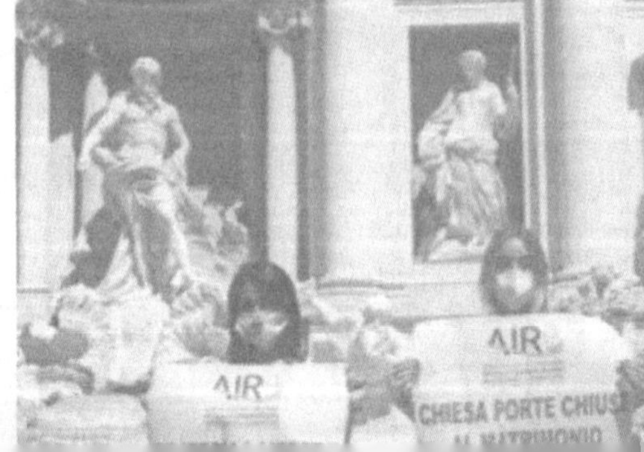

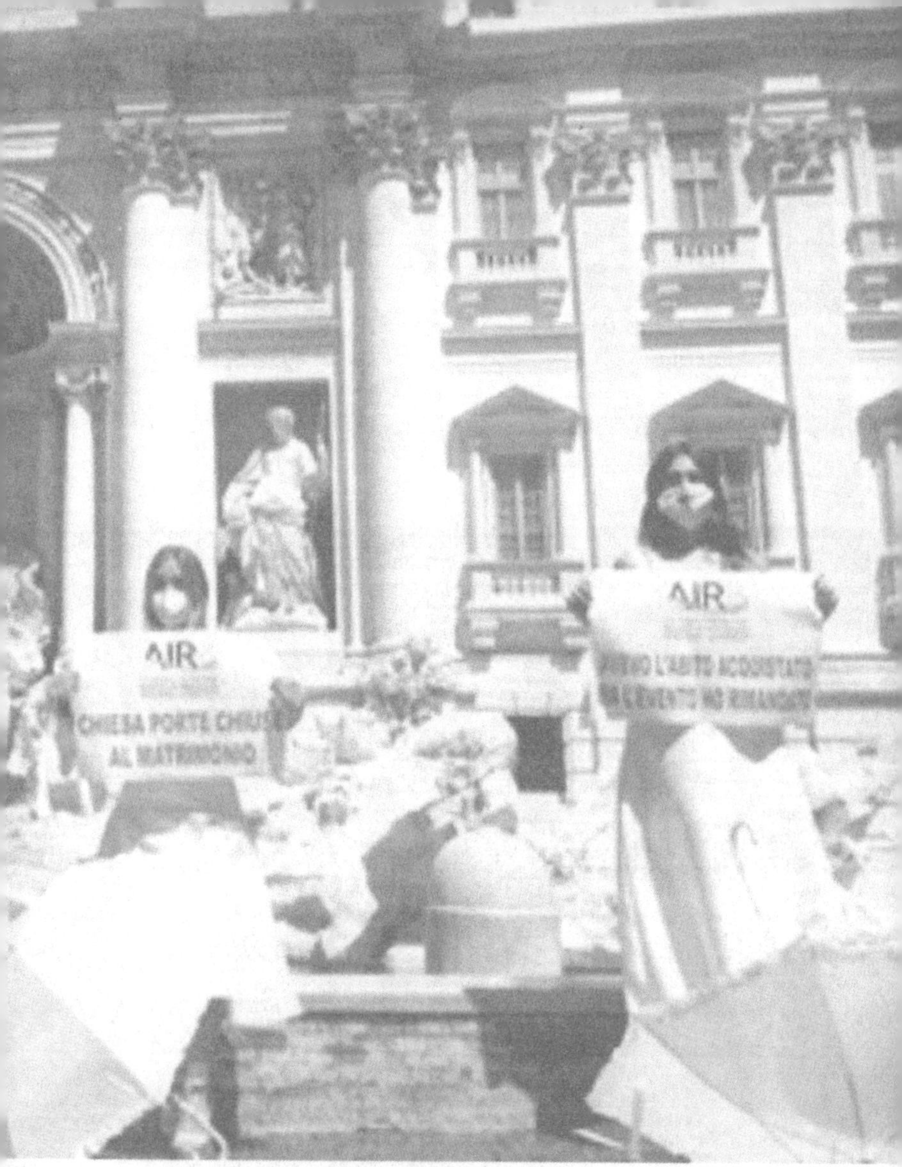

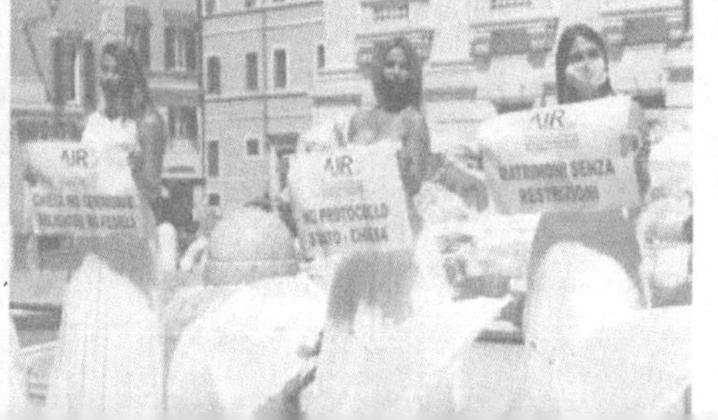
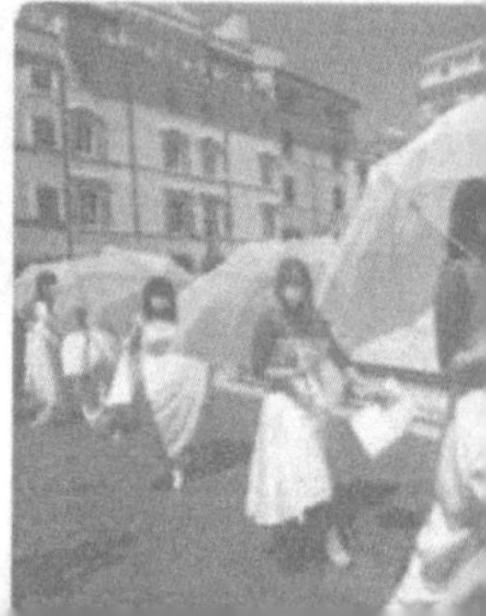

Bonus Mat

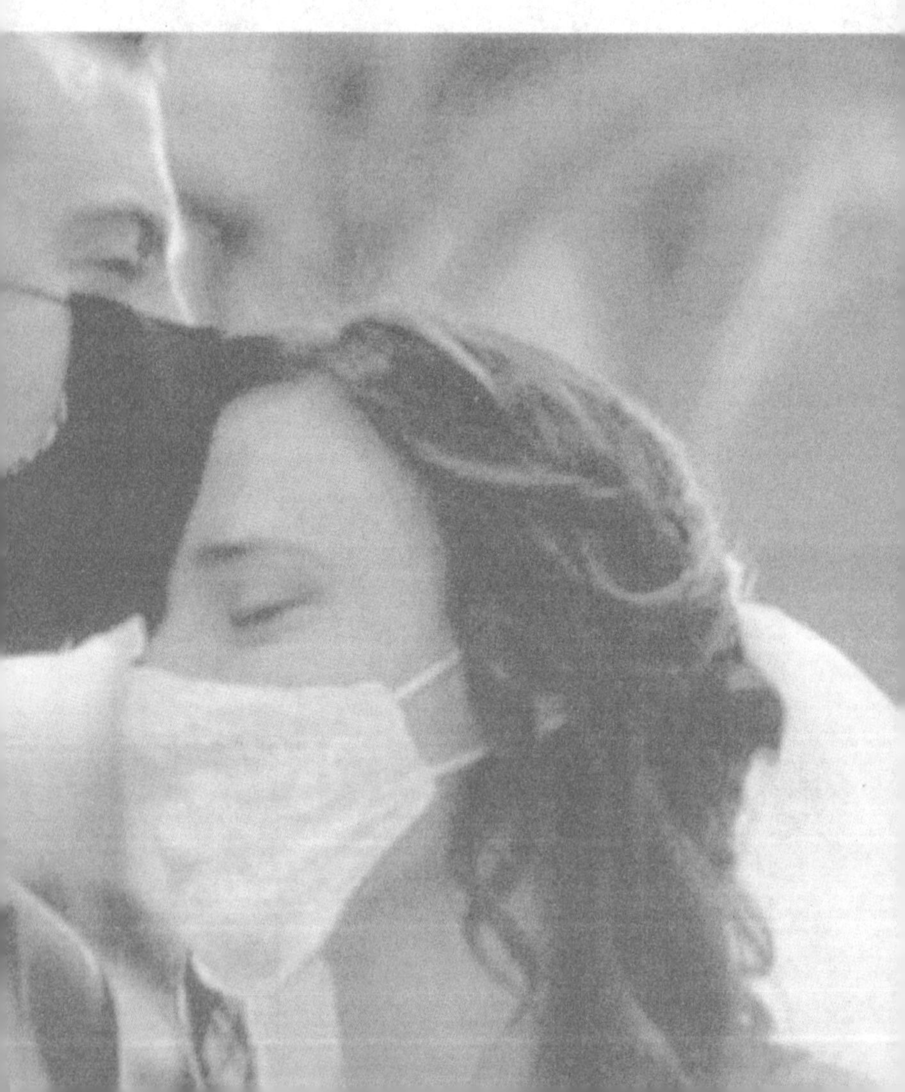

imoni 2020

1.203

82   *Protest of restaurant owners in Milan, in front of Arco della Pace, Aprin 6, 2020.* The demonstration was held in support of the restaurant sector following the decree of October 24 that requires the closure of activities at 6 pm. With the Decree of the President of the Council of Ministers of October 24, 2020 "Further urgent measures to cope with the epidemiological emergency from COVID-19" time restrictions were imposed on restaurant activities. Following the new provisions, 6 petitions were launched on the online platform change.org, between October 25 and 27, 2020, whose prerogative was the reopening of restaurants beyond the hours established by the new DPCM. All the petitions, addressed to the President of the Council, reached, on November 13, 2020, a number of signatures equal to 7,833.

86   *Potest "Bauli in Piazza" of entertainment workers in Milan, in Piazza del Duomo, October 11, 2020.* Demonstration in support of entertainment workers severely harmed by provisions introduced during 2020 to contain the SARS-CoV-2 pandemic. With the proclamation of the state of emergency for COVID-19 on January 22, 2020, the first measures to contain the contagion were implemented throughout Italy. These were followed during 2020 by decree-laws that, for the entire period of the pandemic, suspended shows open to the public in theaters, concert halls and cinemas as well as fairs and events of any kind except those held remotely. In support of the entertainment workers most affected by these measures, 14 online petitions were launched on the change.org platform from February 2020 to November 13, 2020. All petitions, directed to national institutions, reached a number of signatures of 83,956.

90   *Protest of taxi drivers in Naples, in Piazza del Plebiscito, October 27, 2020.* Taxi drivers protest against the measures introduced by the DPCM of October 24. During the emergency period, to protect the health of taxi drivers, two online petitions were launched on the change.org platform. These addressed to national and regional institutions, were supported on November 13, 2020 by 218 signatures.

96   *Protest of riders in Milan, November 5, 2020.* Riders take to the streets to protest against the agreement signed on September 16 between AssoDelivery, the association representing the main companies in the home food delivery sector—Deliveroo, Glovo, Just Eat, Social Food and Uber Eats—and the UGL (General Labor Union) union. Although the changes made to the riders' contracts guarantee minimum wages, night, holiday and night-time allowances, they frame these as self-employed workers. As a result, the protections afforded to employees, such as vacation and sick leave, are not guaranteed. These conditions are part of a historical period in which home delivery is destined to increase due to the restrictive measures introduced to contain contagions. No online petitions were launched on the change.org platform in support of riders during the health emergency period from January 22 to November 13, 2020.

98 *Demostration of nurses in Milan, in front of Palazzo del Consiglio Regionale della Lombardia, to commemorate healthcare personnel who died during the first wave, June 10, 2020.* From March 9 to May 18, 2020, dates marking the beginning and end of the first Italian lockdown, for economic and personal protection against contagion of healthcare personnel, 37 online petitions were launched on the change.org platform. These, addressed to national and regional government institutions, reached 1,973,455 signatures on November 13, 2020.

102 *Protest of ceremony workers in Rome, in front of Trevi Fountain, July 7, 2020.* The demonstration was held in support of the industry that organizes wedding ceremonies and parties and against the suspension of religious ceremonies due to the pandemic. On May 18 with the end of the first nationwide lockdown and the arrival of the summer season, 2 petitions were launched to restore and reward weddings in times of pandemic. These petitions, addressed to national government institutions, were supported by 1,210 signatures on November 13, 2020.

Body as a Medium: On the Contemporary (De)Generation of Transcendent Spaces

Malvina Borgherini

INCARNATION OF THE SUPERNATURAL

In 1223 in Alatri (today in the Italian province of Frosinone), a girl grieving over an unrequited love goes to a witch who suggests she obtain a host during the next Eucharistic rite, with which she will prepare a love potion. The young girl goes to church and, after receiving her communion, holds the consecrated host in her mouth; having hidden it in a piece of cloth, she takes it home to give it to the witch. After three days, the young girl discovers that the bread has turned into a piece of human flesh. Regretting her sacrilege, she admits to what happened and gives the piece of flesh, still bleeding, to the bishop.

The event, using a term dear to Károly Kerényi, assumes the features of a *technicized myth* (that is, a story which by virtue of its charm, whether true or false, is able to mobilize the masses). This takes shape—with the timing proper of an excellent advertisement campaign—only a few years after the Fourth Council of the Lateran of 1215, the synod in which the Church introduces in the Catholic doctrine the term "transubstantiation," to indicate and define the Eucharistic celebration, during which, at the moment of consecration, the body and blood of Christ are incarnated in the bread and the wine.

SPACES, BODIES, COMMUNITIES IN ANTITHESIS

In the *predella* of Urbino called *The Miracle of the Desecrated Host* (1467–68), Paolo Uccello narrates, in six episodes, a story that happened in Paris in 1290. Commissioned by the confraternity of the Corpus Domini of Urbino, the sequence of images tells of a host that is exchanged, which becomes (and looks like) a coin, which bleeds like a body; and of the two communities it pits against each other: Christians and Jews.

In the first episode a woman sells a consecrated host to a Jewish moneylender. In the second, the Jew and his family, after having put the host on the fire, witness its miraculous bleeding which attracts armed gendarmes. In the third, the host is consecrated again. In the fourth the sacrilegious woman is hanged. In the fifth the Jew and his family are burned at the stake. In the last episode, angels and demons—throughout the centuries the images of the latter have been gradually scraped by believers in the apotropaic attempt to ward off evil—fight over the soul of the woman.[1]

---

1   See Jean Louis Schefer, *L'hostie profanée. Histoire d'une fiction théologique* (Paris: POL, 2007).

Told in the *Nuova Cronica* written by Giovanni Villani in the first decades of the fourteenth century,[2] the story is evidence of the renewed attempt to force Italy's Jews into an antithetical spatiality around the middle of the fifteenth century. That time was the beginning of the Monte di pietà (Mounts of piety), financial institutions created by some monastic orders to manage low entity loans, with the goal of taking the place of Jewish bankers. In Urbino, the Monte di pietà was established in 1468 with the blessing of countess Battista Sforza, wife of Federico da Montefeltro.

ON RITUALITY AND ON THE PROCESSES OF EXCHANGE

Fernando Martins de Bulhões, known throughout his life as friar Anthony of Lisbon and later as Saint Anthony, died in Padua on June 13, 1231. Famous for his miracles and speeches, he was canonized only one year after his death. The church built to preserve his remains and venerate his relics—known simply as *il Santo*, "the Saint"—has been a pilgrimage destination

---

2   Giovanni Villani, *Nuova cronica* VIII, 143, ed. Giuseppe Porta, I, (Omegna [VB]: Fondazione Pietro Bembo-Guanda, 1990), 616–17).

for almost eight hundred years. On October 10, 1991 three men, armed and masked, stole Saint Anthony's chin; the news has an immediate planetary echo, but it will take time before knowing that the man who ordered the *abduction* was Felice Maniero, at the time boss of the Brenta mafia.[3] In exchange for the return of the relic, the demands are the release of the boss' cousin Giuliano Rampin, and the repeal of the special surveillance measure applied to Felice Maniero: a piece of a dead man's body for the freedom of two living ones.

Despite, little by little, the dead cease to exist, "rejected by the symbolic circulation of the group," a small provincial gangster is able to reintegrate them in their role of "fully fledged beings, worthy exchange partners."[4] What changes here is the interstitial figure which comes between the living and the dead, the mediator in the exchange process, those who hold control and power:

3   Maniero's intentions was to have the saint's tongue stolen, a relic both more iconic and famous than his chin. Because of the public's strong reaction and having nonetheless obtained the attention of the parties with whom he wanted to negotiate—the forces of law and order—the boss of the *mala del Brenta* (Brenta Mafia) did not go after his sloppy henchmen. See the interview with Felice Maniero that appeared on the dossier *Il Santo ritrovato 1991–2011* (Nicoletta Masetto, "Un boss non è un eroe," Messaggero di Sant'Antonio 193 (October 2011): 44–47).

4   Jean Baudrillard, *Lo scambio simbolico e la morte*, trans. Girolamo Mancuso (Milano: Feltrinelli, 1979), 139. Original edition: *L'Échange symbolique et la mort* (Paris: Gallimard, 1976).

no longer the servants of the church, but the forces of law and order. Forces that, later, starting from what happened in July 2001 during the demonstrations organized by the Genoa Social Forum[5] to challenge the G8 summit, enacted extremely subtle forms of control. What in Genoa was meant to be an alliance of bodies became a battleground with one deceased, two hundred and fifty arrested and over a thousand wounded. By instilling the germ of fear, that tragic display immediately emptied the streets.

Rituals are symbolic acts. They represent, and pass on, the values and orders on which a community is based. They bring forth a *community without communication*; today, however, *communication without community* prevails. Rituals are constituted by *symbolic percep-*

5   The Genoa Social Forum (GSF) was created in 2000 as a network of movements, parties, associations and no global civil societies (more than 1187 different organizations, both national and international took part in it). Through spokespeople Vittorio Agnoletto and Luca Casarini, the GSF demanded the annulment of the G8 Summit, as the reunion of the heads of state and heads of government was considered unlawful, since a handful of powerful men were taking decisions that would have impacted peoples that were not represented by the G8, and because the interdiction from freely entering the red zone—the city had been divided in zones of different colours by law enforcement—constituted a limitation of the constitutional freedoms. In those days those very freedoms were significantly harmed: with beatings, threats and torture at the expense of helpless and peaceful demonstrators. For a synthesis of the events of July 2001 see Carlo Lucarelli's documentary, G8 Genova, made by RAI 3.

tion. Symbol (Greek: *symbolon*) originally referred to the sign of recognition
between guest-friends (*tessera hospitalis*).
One guest-friend broke a clay tablet in
two, kept one half for himself and gave
the other half to another as a sign of
guest-friendship. Thus, a symbol serves
the purpose of recognition.[6]

Among the words that open a recent essay by
Byung-Chul Han—a text "not driven by the
poignant desire to go back to rites," rather in
which a "genealogy of their disappearance"
takes shape[7]—some sensible pairs immediately
catch the eye: rites/actions (symbolic), commu-
nity/communication, host/symbol. And a myth
comes to mind: that told by Aristophanes in
Plato's *Symposium*[8] on the original nature of
humankind, when human beings were round
and had two faces, four arms and four legs,
and two sexes. Cut in half by Zeus to stem
his exuberance, man is since then a *symbolon*
with the incessant need to be reunited with
his missing part (*symballein* in Greek namely
means "to put together"). "Rites are, in this

114

6   Byung-Chul Han, *The disappearance of rituals. A topology of the present-polity*,
     trans. Daniel Steuer (Cambridge: Polity Press, 2020), 1. Original edition: *Von
     Verschwinden der Rituale. Eine Topologie der Gegenwart* (Berlin: Ullstein, 2019).
7   Ibid., 9.
8   Plato, *Symposium*, 189D-193E. See Platone. *Tutti gli scritti*, ed. Giovanni Reale
     (Milano: Rusconi, 1994), 499–503.

sense, also a symbolic practice, a practice of *symballein*, insofar they reunite people and create a bond, a whole, a community."[9]

The symbolic action implies recognition: we are not seeing something new, but rather something we already know, which continues to occur over time, which has a duration. And in turn the recognition gives place to the process of human "settling."[10] Rites transform the being-in-the-world into a *being-at-home*, make the world a more comfortable place, give life stability. To use the words of Antoine de Saint-Exupéry,

> rites are in time what home is in space. [...] It is well that time is a construct. In this way we can go on from name-day to name-day, from birthday to birthday, from vintage to vintage, like I did as a child walking from the council chamber to the silent chamber, between the thick walls of my father's palace, in which every step made sense.[11]

---

9 Han, *The disappearance of rituals. A topology of the present-polity*, 16.
10 Gadamer, in defining this process, states that he uses the Hegelian term "Einhausung" ("settling down"). Hans Georg Gadamer, *L'attualità del bello*, trans. Riccardo Dottori and Livio Bottani (Genova: Marietti, 1988), 51 ; See Han, *The disappearance of rituals. A topology of the present-polity*, 11–12.
11 Ibid., 13 ; Antoine de Saint-Exupéry, *Cittadella*, trans. Ezio L. Gaya (Roma: Borla, 1999), 24.

The ritual community is a corporation: the orders and values of a community—through rites, genuine acts of incarnation—are physically experienced and consolidated; inscribed in the body, incorporated, internalized through the body.

It is from the very limbs of the bodies, or from objects related to them, owned by those around which a particular community has formed—the Christian one—that some of the most ancient ritual places have emerged: churches. Churches as communities that echo the words and actions of a god, incarnated in the body of a man born of a woman that had never laid with a man; a god-man whose body and blood—during the Eucharistic celebration—turn into bread and wine, to feed his believers. Churches as spaces in which bones, blood, fingers, tongues, eyes, spines, nails, pieces of wood, shrouds, that is, remains of corpses or objects tied to the death, are reanimated in the gathering of a community and in the reactivation of processes of exchange between the living and the dead. Rites which create axes of resonance: vertical, towards the otherworldly; horizontal, in civil society; diagonal, in relation to things. Processes of exchange which, differently from what happens in other communities in which the relationship between the living and the dead takes the shape of a social (and direct) act,[12] happen through the mediation of a group which becomes the holder of the power: the clergy. For the Sara people of Chad—a community stranger to Western traditions—facts of life such as birth, illness and death are devoid of sense because they cannot be exchanged symbolically, and only through initiation processes are they able to transcend the absolute disorder that these natural events could cause.[13] The initiation does not mean to pit life *against* death, towards a rebirth: "it is the *split* of life and death that the initiation wards off,"[14] and it is on this split, on the breaking of the union between the living and the dead, on the breaking of the exchange of life and death, on the interdic-

12 Here I am referring to the experience by French ethnologist Robert Jaulin, who lived among the Sara people of Chad between 1954 and 1959, which he recounted in his *La Mort Sara. L'ordre de la vie ou la pensée de la mort au Tchad* (Paris: Union générale d'éditions, 1971). See also Vittorio Lanternari and Rosa Teresa Di Paolo, "Intervista a un etnologo 'scomodo'. Robert Jaulin," *Lares* 51, no. 2 (April-June 1985): 223–47.

13 An initiation process, for example, happens when the Sara ancestors symbolically kill the Koy (the young ones of the group), which are later left in the hands of their initiation parents who teach them, cure them and educate them (through an initiation rebirth). Or when, through the offer of food, a brother offers a wife to a deceased member of the family thereby bringing him back to life and including him in the group's daily life; and all of this with a mutual exchange: because the deceased himself offers his wife, the clan's land, to a living member of his family, with the goal of coming back to life by assimilating with him, and bringing him back to life by assimilating him with himself. See Baudrillard, *Lo scambio simbolico e la morte*, 144.

14 Ibid., 145.

tion of death and the dead, that the very first emergency point of social control is established.[15] "Priestly power is based on the monopoly of death and on the exclusive control of the relationships with the dead. The dead are the first domain reserved, and given back to the exchange through a forced mediation: that of the priests."[16]

RITUAL: OR ON THE COMMUNITY SPACE OF THE SACRED INCARNATE

The *Messe pour un corps* (1969) by Michel Journiac first happened on November 6, 1969 at the Daniel Templon Gallery in Paris, transformed into a place of worship for the occasion and fitted with an altar covered in white linen, candles, chalice, paten, etc. Here, the artist, dressed like a priest, recites a mass in Latin for those who have gathered, and at the end of the rite offers a special host for the communion: a pudding the main ingredient of which is his blood.

Journiac, who as a youngster studied in a seminar, articulates in this action his interest for religion: "an alliance—this is how he defines it—between man and sacred, in the

118

15   Ibid., 142.
16   Ibid., 143.

body of a man, in a human body [...] Humanity had invented something that freed it and from which nobody could be excluded."[17] *Messe pour un corps* is a moment of union: by offering his blood, symbol of life and the incarnation of a god, Journiac opens a space for sharing between the individual (the viewer) and his possibility to fuse with the otherworldly (essence of the communion rite). And at the same time it is an act of provocation, a blasphemous act which questions the powers that be.

CEREMONY AS A HOME:
OR ON THE CELEBRATION
OF THE FUNERAL RITE

"The pre-history of my relationship with cinema involves also my mother's sexophobia and her fear of germs."[18] Cecilia Mangini's passion for cinema takes the moves of her mother's hypochondria, who considered the movie theater a place of sexual perdition and bacterial contamination. For Mangini, cinema was a beautiful and forbidden world from which she had

---

17 Audrey Dubouch, *Art corporel et art sociologique: de la violence sauvage à la violence barbare*, dissertation on Aesthetics, supervisor J.-L. Palmier, Université Paris I Panthéon-Sorbonne (October 1993), 31.

18 Mirko Grasso, "Il cinema e il mondo. Conversazione con Cecilia Mangini," in Stendalì. *Canti e immagini della morte nella Grecia salentina* (Copertino [LE]: Kurumuny, 2006), 45.

been incomprehensibly excluded: the only exception was Florence's Supercinema (the theater had a moving ceiling, opened at each show for ventilation, thus her mother considered it, if not healthy, at least a bit less epidemic). And the attempt to defend her from an invisible evil, catalyst element in the creation of an alliance of bodies, will become a recurrent theme in her works.

In *Stendalì (Suonano ancora)*, a 1960 film which documents the expressions of pain which accompany the death of a teenager, Mangini brings an ancient Salentine funeral right back to life. This rite is structured in songs, laments and specific body movements, from the head to the hands which wave white handkerchiefs. "The honor of crying as a tribute to the deceased [...] constitutes a unifying moment in an archaic society which finds the sense of its existence and the will to leave its own memory even in situations as tragic as death."[19] The birth of a community of survival, a ceremony as home, allows for the accommodation of a celebration of pain due to the loss of another mother: Pasolini's. The poet, author of the accompanying text to Mangini's images, joins the late lamented through the recreation of these folk songs.

120

19   Mirko Grassi, "Premessa," in *Ibid.*, 15.

Sixty years later and through a mostly static camera, Carl Olsson, in his *Meanwhile on Earth* (2020), narrates the freezing and *sanitary* funeral rites of northern Europe. The documentary—a caustic and elegiac work on the Swedish funeral industry—reveals, in the constant visual absence of the body of the deceased, the community of those who work around the funeral, marking the change between rite and production.

THE OTHER'S BODY, SEDUCTION AND PORNOGRAPHY

Between July 19 and 22, 1983, on a stage space in Munich, Harun Farocki filmed the shooting of the picture of the Playmate of the Month, to be printed on the central pages of "Playboy." The magazine, mostly renowned for photo shoots depicting women in the nude, talks about a certain lifestyle (culture, sports, cars...) around which millions of dollars revolve. In *Ein Bild* the look of the director is evidence of the care, seriousness and responsibility of the people who are creating an image of such importance: one can see—Farocki says— that they are as careful "as they would be if they were splitting Uranium."[20] A naked body at the center of a commercial cosmos, an invisible point of an infinite galaxy, is filmed. And the playful power of seduction, through a process of progressive distancing, is rekindled: a power which does not aim to repress, but engage with the other in "a kind of open strategy game, in which things might be overturned."[21]

A scenic and playful distance, the desire and fantasy for the *other* are constituent forms of seduction: it is this reciprocity that characterizes the game with power.

The compulsion to produce, today's leitmotif, touches upon all aspects of life, including sexuality. The etymology of the word "produce"—from Latin *producere*, which means "carrying forward, presenting to a public, display for sale"—is in itself close the meaning of the term "pornography"—from Greek πόρνη, "prostitute" and -γραφία, derivate of γράφω, "writing, drawing, study"—a term that in its strict sense refers to the "images (or texts) about prostitutes" and, in its modern, broader sense to "images of sex (or of the sexual act) displayed for sale." No

122

---

20   See www.harunfarocki.de/de/filme/1980er/1983/ein-bild.html.
21   Michel Foucault, *Antologia. L'impazienza della libertà*, trans. Sabrina Loriga (Milano: Feltrinelli, 2005), 251.

longer a hidden sexuality, acted quietly: its portrayal and its display make it production.

The explicit representation of sexual acts or organs puts a strain on seduction: in pornography, the other is eliminated. Pornographic pleasure is narcissistic, solitary, derives from immediate consumption of a body-object, exposed without veils. Porn becomes, paradoxically, a manifestation of transparency: the free access to what is usually hidden, a super exposition of flesh, a "pornographic overproduction of sex," destroy sexuality and eroticism more efficiently than morals and repression.[22] The preference for uniqueness, the discomfort caused by ambiguity or ambivalence, the difficulty to access phenomena such as mysteries or secrets, seems to have become characteristic features of our daily lives: are we living in the age of porn?

22 Han, *The disappearance of rituals. A topology of the present-polity*, 117–22.

Contemporary States of Crisis: Migration, Climate Change and COVID-19

Elena Giacomelli, Pierluigi Musarò

Times of crises and emergencies can provide stark reminders of the importance of language and communication. "Emergency" and "crisis" are nowadays the primary terms for referring to catastrophes, conflicts, and settings for human suffering.[1] Digging into the etymology of words, we can see emergency as an "unforeseen occurrence requiring immediate attention," while crisis can be intended as "an unstable situation, in political, social, economic or military affairs, especially one involving an impending abrupt change." From this perspective, an emergency appears to be a sudden and unpredictable event emerging in a background of usual normality, causing danger and suffering and demanding immediate action. Hence, the word "emergency" points to what happens without reference to causes, agency or any other specific outcomes, depoliticizing the issue itself.[2]

Usage of such words is often secular. Deployment of terms such as "emergency" and "crisis" focuses the attention on the immediate event, and not on its causes.

---

1   Didier Fassin and Mariella Pandolfi, *Contemporary states of emergency: The politics of military and humanitarian interventions* (New York: Zone Book, 2010).

2   Craig Calhoun, "A World of Emergencies: Fear, Intervention, and the Limits of Cosmopolitan Order," *Canadian Review of Sociology and Anthropology* 41, no. 4 (2004): 373–395.

It calls for an urgent response, usually humanitarian or military, with no time for economic, social or political complex analysis.[3] Framing migration, climate change and COVID-19 with crisis narratives translate into, and justifies, *ad hoc* and short-term responses instead of holistic approaches that may be more appropriate given the systemic, global, and political nature of these topics.

The choice of how we communicate is never neutral. It conveys differences in the representation of the world and plays a major role in the re-production, re-creation and transformation of meanings and in the social construction of reality.[4] While choosing appropriate words to describe phenomena can help us to understand them and to manage them better, using inaccurate or distorted words could mislead not only the understanding of events, but also emotions, decisions and actions that follow. What are the consequences of associating the words "crisis" and "emergency" to long-term (political) events such as climate

126

<hr>

3   Craig Calhoun, "The Idea of Emergency: Humanitarian Action and Global (Dis)Order," in *Contemporary states of emergency: The politics of military and humanitarian interventions*, ed. Didier Fassin and Mariella Pandolfi (New York: Zone Book, 2010), 18–39.

4   Peter L. Berger and Thomas Luckmann, *The Social Construction of Reality: A Treatise in the Sociology of Knowledge* (New York: Doubleday & Company, 1966).

change and migration? Which are the consequences of this normalization of emergencies? What happens when we have a complex Russian nesting doll situation, a concatenation of crises, such as the one happening with migration, climate change and COVID-19?

In this chapter, we try to answer the aforementioned questions by considering *framing* a useful approach in the analysis of how migration, climate change and COVID-19 have been communicated by the media and translated into policies and practices. The value of a framing approach is in the underlining of the ways in which actors, both unconsciously and intentionally, draw on various cultural aspects to define the boundary of an issue.

According to Goffman,[5] *framing* is the basic process through which individual experiences are interpreted, in which media and communication play a major role. The narrative within a frame can preclude some options, while making others look more reasonable. In this sense, framing is the positioning of issues and messages in a way that influences individual perceptions, public opinion, and policy makers on a phenom-

5   Erving Goffman, *Frame analysis: An essay on the organization of experience* (New York: Harper and Row, Cambridge: Harvard University Press, 1974).

enon. It is the name we give to the process through which we order ideas on complex issues, giving more relevance to certain dimensions over others.[6] Narratives, metaphors and myths, central to a frame, are usually abstract and general in nature and, to have power, must resonate within a particular culture[7] and subculture.[8]

In the last decades, the concept of *framing* has increasingly been utilized in media and communication studies to indicate the selection of "some aspects of a perceived reality and make them more salient in a communicating text, in such a way as to promote a particular problem definition, causal interpretation, moral evaluation, and/or treatment recommendation" for the phenomena described.[9]

In other words, we can affirm that nowadays social actions and phenomena

128

6   Matthew C. Nisbet, "Knowledge into action: framing the debates over climate change and poverty," in *Doing News Framing Analysis: Empirical and Theoretical Perspectives*, ed. Paul D'Angelo and Jim A. Kuypers (London: Routledge, 2010), 43–83.
7   James K. Hertog and Douglas M. McLeod, "A multiperspectival approach to framing analysis: A field guide," in *Framing Public Life: Perspectives on Media and Our Understanding of the Social World*, ed. Stephen D. Reese, Oscar H. Gandy, and August E. Grant (London: Routledge, 2001), 139–161.
8   Hedda Ransan-Cooper et al., "Being(s) framed: The means and ends of framing environmental migrants," *Global Environmental Change*, no. 35 (2015): 106–115.
9   Robert M. Entman, "Framing: toward clarification of a fractured paradigm," *Journal of Communication* 43, no.4 (1993): 52.

are increasingly framed and informed by media technologies and logics orienting people's perceptions and behaviors. As a consequence, drawing on Stig Hjarvard's definition of mediatization as a process in which "the media exert a particularly dominant influence on other institutions,"[10] we cannot avoid highlighting how our ideas of migration and borders, climate change and COVID-19 crises are influenced by the mediatization and spectacularization of these phenomena.

In the last decades, public and political discourses and the (old and new) media framed migration, climate change and the Pandemic through a crisis and emergency narrative. In fact, this sense of suddenness and unpredictability of these phenomena is reinforced by the media. Yet, crises and emergencies are unexpectedly short-term and temporary by nature, whilst climate change, migration and public global health (in relation to COVID-19) are long-term phenomena requiring such policy responses. The next paragraphs analyze how migration, climate change and COVID-19 have all been framed as crises and the consequences of it.

10   Stig Hjarvard, "The mediatization of society: A theory of the media as agents of social and cultural change," *Nordicom Review* 29, no. 2, (2008): 13.

FRAMING CRISIS: INTERRELATION BETWEEN MIGRATION, CLIMATE CHANGE AND COVID-19

Climate change, migration and public health are three interrelated key political, structural and global phenomena of the current period. The significance of these three challenges have been labeled by the media as a situated and circumscribed crisis from an emergency perspective.

What is the interrelation between migration, climate change and COVID-19? In the midst of the COVID-19 crisis, an immediate political response was to the closure of borders and the immobilization of people. As we will analyze in the next paragraphs, the metaphors utilized during the ongoing pandemic justified a systematic search for an *enemy*. This *hunt* found the perfect scapegoats in migrants and foreigners, which helped in the construction of a national *us* as *victims* and the contagion as a *threat* coming from the outside.

Moreover, as we have seen in the first months of the current pandemic, COVID-19 could be tied with climate change, with regards to the positive effects, albeit temporary, of lockdown measures on lowering carbon emission.[11] In addition to this, many radical voices directly link the ongoing pandemic with the environmentally damaging capitalist practices that are also driving climate change. A capitalist system that is failing to find solutions and does not recognize the importance of tackling the causes. Human-driven environmental destruction has widely been found to have led to the conditions that resulted in the global pandemic.[12] The COVID-19 pandemic has exposed the failure to understand the mutually-affective connection between humans and nature.

As mentioned above, in the last decades, migration, climate change, and now COVID-19, are usually framed as *contemporary states of emergency*. An *invasion* by migrants, 2019 as the year of the climate emergency declaration, the war against the invisible enemy (COVID-19): these are just some of the terms commonly used to name these phenomena.

In the contemporary world, even if migration, climate change and pandemics

<hr>

11 Daniel Rosenbloom and Jochen Markard, "A COVID-19 recovery for climate," *Science* 368, no. 6490 (2020): 447.
12 Christine K. Johnson et al., "Global shifts in mammalian population trends reveal key predictors of virus spillover risk," *Proceedings of the Royal Society B: Biological Sciences* 287, no. 1924 (2020): 20192736 ; Drew Pendergrass and Troy Vettese, "The Climate Crisis and COVID-19 Are Inseparable," *Jacobin* (2020), https://jacobinmag.com/2020/05/climate-change-crisis-covid-coronavirus-environment.

are structural, political and long-term events, these have been treated as short-term and circumscribed crises. This led to their political and mediatic manipulation, distorted perceptions of reality, the proliferation of *fake news* and, as a further consequence, generated a climate of uncertainty.

In a historical period governed by fake news, the role of gathering information, analyzing data and the necessity of a re-politicization of words and meanings become essential to prevent fear and alienation, side effects of an alarmist communication of events and a distorted perception of reality.

Through an emergency frame, the following paragraphs analyze how these three political challenges have been de-politicized and translated into the crisis techno-management dominion.

THE EUROPEAN "MIGRATION CRISIS"

Italy has always been characterized by mass emigration. In the last decades, this country transformed into a target for immigration, and specifically, the first migration flows came from North Africa, especially from Morocco, Tunisia and Egypt. Italy belongs to the so-called "Mediterranean Southern

European model of migration"[13] characterized by a lack of immigration policies, a large underground economy attracting undocumented migrants, a strong segmentation of the labor market and the use of regularizations. From 1990 to 2007, eastern European countries accounted for the majority of the migration inflow. From 1996 to 2019, the foreign resident population increased from 737,793 to 5,255,503. When considering non-resident regular and irregular immigrants, this number rises to 6,222,000,[14] equal to 7% of the total population.[15]

Despite irregular immigrants representing only a minority of the total immigrant population, the phenomenon of irregular immigration has received increasing media visibility in recent years. Very visible arrivals, certainly dramatic but also dramatized, took the center stage, obscuring the other, much more relevant components of a complex and multi-faceted universe such as that of migra-

13 Russell King, "Southern Europe in the changing global map of migration," in *Eldorado or Fortress? Migration in Southern Europe*, ed. Russell King, Gabriella Lazaridis, and Charalambos Tsardanidis (Basingstoke: Macmillan, 2000), 1–26.
14 Fondazione ISMU, *Venticinquesimo Rapporto sulle migrazioni 2019* (Milano: FrancoAngeli, 2020).
15 IOM, *World Migration Report 2020* (2020). https://publications.iom.int/books/world-migration-report-2020.

tion.[16] The emphasis on the need to contain the flow does not derive from an objective analysis of the data, but from the impact of this hyper-visibility on public opinion. Moreover, some political actors have fed this situation, making it a matter of controversy and propaganda.[17] In a nutshell, this hyper-mediatization has led to a substantial discrepancy between perception and reality, which has been followed by an increased concern about security and sovereignty.

The media have an important role in influencing political attitudes and in framing public debates towards a concepts of "otherness,"[18] migration and asylum. In the last decade, the discursive practices and representation strategies have been framing irregular migrants crossing borders as a widespread *emergency* to be managed in terms of a social, cultural and political *crisis* at a national and European level. Far outstripping any real crisis is the public anxiety about migration and asylum-seeking in Europe, which in part has grown due to

134

---

16   Pierluigi Musarò and Paola Parmiggiani, "Beyond black and white: the role of media in portraying and policing migration and asylum in Italy," *International Review of Sociology* 27, no. 2 (2017): 241–260.

17   Maurizio Ambrosini, *L'invasione immaginaria. L'immigrazione oltre i luoghi comuni* (Roma: Laterza, 2020).

18   Pierre Bourdieu, *Le sens pratique* (Paris: Minuit, 1980).

the media coverage of the phenomenon, as well as the rhetoric of politicians, who describe Europe as being *invaded* by people fleeing conflict or seeking a better life.[19]

The duration of the so-called *migration crisis* created a climate of fear and uncertainty, which fueled a vicious circle in which the media influenced and shaped the citizens' understanding of the phenomena, as well as policies on migration and asylum.

Institutional and political actors have mirrored public anxieties and security concerns, endorsing emergency narratives, aggressive policing and the militarization of borders. Unable to engage with citizens' concerns, they have helped to conflate migration with insecurity, creating a fertile breeding ground for xenophobic and populist reactions. As a consequence of this *politics of fear*, the number of anti-immigrant and anti-Muslim parties in Europe increased.[20] And there is today a strong consensus on a hard line on migration, calls for the shutting of borders, and even stricter policies.

---

19   Ed. Paola Barretta, *Notizie senza approdo. Settimo Rapporto Carta di Roma* (2019). http://www.cartadiroma.org/osservatorio/rapporti/.
20   Ruth Wodak, *The politics of fear. What right-wing discourses mean* (London: Sage, 2015).

In line with this widespread feeling, the so-called *migration crisis* marks a crucial juncture in Italian politics as well. It is not a surprise that the fifty-second report by the social and economic research institute CENSIS published in 2018 depicts Italy as suffering from fear of the future and of migrants, using the term "psychic sovereignism," meaning a generalized and sorrowful sense of loss of national sovereignty, accompanied by an upsurge of fear of the *other*, beginning with immigrants. The fifty-third edition (2019), also shows that almost 7 out of 10 Italians believe that hate, intolerance, and racism towards minorities in the country has risen over the past year.

Throughout this year, in Italy, the spread of COVID-19 has contributed to fueling a surge in anti-immigrant sentiments. Notwithstanding the negative shift in coverage tone, migration in online media worldwide has been associated with the spread of the virus. In light of such fear, the government closed its borders and introduced social distancing measures during quarantine. As things took a catastrophic turn in Italy, public expressions of concern and mistrust towards migrants followed. Their suffering has been ignored; their histories are truly not taken into account. Under the strain of COVID-19, populism has made their suffering more invisible, and in places like the United States or Italy, this has emphasized the threat element in which migrants are seen as carriers of the virus.

This condition of ongoing pandemic opens up a new space for reflection and critique of the populist imagery. The boundaries between solidarity and surveillance keep shifting, contracting and expanding, as fear implodes and anger explodes among Italians. The Pandemic forced us to redraw boundaries of our possible trajectories and re-framed migration crisis discourses. The COVID-19 pandemic and the fear of the *other* has shifted the discourse on migration, shedding light on how, during the Pandemic, the news have been polarized: on one side, the closing of borders due to the connection between migration and illness; on the other, the regularization of migrants working in the informal economy.[21]

2019 CLIMATE "EMERGENCY"

Studies on the media coverage of climate change issues have demonstrated the signifi-

21 Elena Giacomelli, Pierluigi Musarò, and Paola Parmiggiani, "The 'invisible enemy' and the usual suspects. How COVID-19 re-framed migration in Italian media representations," in *Sociologia della Comunicazione* (Milano: FrancoAngeli, 2020).

cant role of the media in determining public opinion and the shaping of new climate policies. In order to communicate effectively on climate change, it is crucial to know how people understand this phenomenon. Recognizing which frame is given to climate change helps us to understand how communication shapes not only what we know and think about it, but also what we do about it. Or, in Greta Thunberg's words,[22] what we don't do about it.

In the past few years, the increased media attention of the climate *emergency* emphasizes the decisive role of crisis narratives as perceived *turning points*. In 2019, the "climate emergency" was declared.[23] This led to immediate action and concrete responses such as the youth movements Extinction Rebellion and Fridays For Future, to the fight against an urgent threat.

Yet, as crises are meant to be temporary in nature, the use of this term with regards to climate change can be quite problematic,[24] mainly for two sets of problems. First,

138

22 https://www.nationalobserver.com/2019/09/28/features/mighty-greta-motivates-massive-montreal-climate-march.
23 https://climateemergencydeclaration.org/climate-emergency-declarations-cover-15-million-citizens/.
24 Mustafa Abbas, "Climate change as a global political issue," *Atoms for Peace an International Journal* 3, no. 3 (2012): 219–237.

climate change necessitates a long-term approach, such as structural changes in lifestyle. Framing climate change as an emergency has several potential disadvantages. Patrick Hodder and Brian Martin[25] claim that this emergency framing may be counterproductive as it does not help in building popular support for long-term efforts, and it can disempower citizens, presenting the problem as too big, whereas providing practical opportunities for action is a better long-term approach. As pointed out in the Eco Media 2019 Report,[26] it is essential that environmental sustainability issues shouldn't only be relegated to emergencies, such as weather and natural disasters, but should have a wider, more visible and constant space that can feed a general virtuous emulative circle. Secondly, whilst the environmental crisis may be global, its impact is not felt in the same way everywhere. Due to the political nature of the issue, a first analysis of media narratives talking about climate change revealed a lack of information on its causes. Most news outlets tend

25 Patrick Hodder and Brian Martin, "Climate Crisis? The Politics of Emergency Framing," *Economic and Political Weekly* 44, no. 36 (2009): 55–60.
26 https://www.osservatorio.it/wp-content/uploads/2016/07/Rapporto-Eco-Media-2019-depliant-ricerca.pdf.

to frame climate change discourses just as consequences of serious fast-onset disasters and adaptation strategies. Framing environmental problems just through adaptation can be problematic, as it risks depoliticizing the issue and absolving governments of their responsibilities.[27] Bettini and Gioli questions this assumption:

> Such an articulation is far from unproblematic, not least as, at the end of the day, it shifts the responsibility (for successful adaptation, for survival) onto the vulnerable. It represents an attempt to individualize climate adaptation in ways that extend a series of neoliberal economic relations that reproduce the conditions out of which vulnerabilities emerge.[28]

Finally, studies conducted underline how climate change is mainly reported as natural disasters and catastrophes, rather than slow-onset environmental change. Slow-onset environmental changes (e.g. desertification,

140

---

27 Alex Flavell, Andrea Milan, and Susanne Melde, "Migration, environment and climate change: Literature review," in *First report in the Migration, environment and climate change series* (Dessau-Roßlau: Umweltbundesamt, 2020).
28 Giovanni Bettini and Giovanna Gioli, "Waltz with development: insights on the developmentalization of climate-induced migration," *Migration and Development* 5, no. 2 (2016): 16.

sea-level rise, land degradation) are seldom considered from a crisis perspective both by the general public and by media outlets, and not considered as part of the environmental problem and climate change as a whole.

To tackle the crisis, greater awareness and more accurate information is needed. Not merely by reporting on episodic news of the destruction of the Italian territory, but by promoting a broader vision, capable of embracing the phenomenon in its entirety and in its global reach. It is necessary to encourage greater media coverage of the issue, able to effectively communicate the urgency and imperative of this situation, which is now a global emergency and requires explaining to the citizenry the risk that is being taken, and to consistently communicate information on individual behaviors and life-styles that can help reduce global warming.

2020 COVID-19 CRISIS

The context of COVID-19 is characterized by high levels of uncertainty and anxiety, mainly caused by the reporting on mortality statistics and daily infections, and the characterization of the crisis as *unprecedented*, which led to a spread of fake news. The current scenario is characterized by total insecurity, where the health emergency is causing other types of emergencies, such as psychological, economic, social and political ones. As if in a dark and unpredictable episode of British TV show Black Mirror, we're underestimating the danger of linking the COVID-19 pandemic with a widespread infodemic—an overabundance of information, not always accurate—and phobocracy—the power exercised through prolonged alarm.Pandemics are not merely serious public health concerns, but rather can trigger terrible socio-economic and political crises in the infected countries. As with past pandemics, COVID-19, apart from becoming the greatest threat to global public health of the century, can also be considered an indicator of social inequality.[29] In his new book, Frank M. Snowden underlines how:

> Epidemic diseases are not random events that afflict societies capriciously and without warning [...] On the contrary, every society produces its own specific vulnerabilities. To study them is to understand that society's structure, its standard of living, and its political priorities.[30]

142

---

29 Indranil Chakraborty and Prasenjit Maity, "COVID-19 outbreak: Migration, effects on society, global environment and prevention," *The Science of the Total Environment* (2020).

30 Frank M. Snowden, *Epidemics and Society: From the Black Death to the Present* (New Haven: Yale University Press; London, 2019).

The use of a *crisis* narrative into this ongoing pandemic has led to war metaphors and the search for an *invisible enemy*. As COVID-19 swept across the world, politicians, news, social media and (even) journalists have chosen, by no means accidentally, to personify COVID-19 as an invisible enemy, adopting war metaphors to narrate the challenges we are facing.

Words matter: Donald Trump started using the phrase "Chinese Virus" in his public statements, giving it a name that attributed and denounced its origin, and consequently giving China a form of responsibility. Through this process of *framing*, Trump tried to shift the focus away from his administration's responsibilities (and failures) in regards to the Pandemic by zeroing in on China.

In her report, Stefania Spina[31] analyzes different linguistic choices made by 6,685 articles published online by the Italian press[32] to address the emergency. Although in slightly different proportions, the majority of them used military metaphors, pervasive war-related terminologies and a constant

31 http://www.treccani.it/magazine/lingua_italiana/articoli/scritto_e_parlato/peste.html.
32 La Repubblica, La Stampa, Il Giornale, Libero, Il Foglio, and Huffington Post.

state of alert, which may lead to fear, panic[33] and even psychosis.[34]

During the COVID-19 crisis, national health services and doctors have become *heroes*, working on the *frontline* fighting the *invisible enemy*. As war is inherently divisive, the metaphor of war divides communities. In fact, while highly appealing as a tool of political rhetoric, war metaphors hide several risks that, in the case of the Pandemic, are extremely dangerous. As Federico Faloppa[35] highlighted, by analyzing the semantic field of this narrative, depicting citizens as simple soldiers and doctors and nurses as "soldiers on the frontlines" reflects the idea of an (invisible) enemy that needs to be fought, a "free for all" battle, where the threat may hide everywhere and within everyone. Such rhetoric succeeded in undermining the feeling of community and creating a trench between *us* and *them*, reducing security to mere control and framing reality by perpetuating the friend/enemy dichotomy.[36] As a

33 https://www.liberoquotidiano.it/news/italia/13570061/coronavirus-mappa-nume-ro-contagi-impressionante-onda-lunga-incubazione-settimana-decisiva.html.

34 https://www.liberoquotidiano.it/news/italia/13569151/vittorio-feltri-drit-to-e-rovescio-milano-nord-coronavirus-stufi-emergenza.html.

35 Federico Faloppa, *#Odio. Manuale di resistenza alla violenza delle parole* (Milano: Utet, 2020).

36 World Bank, *COVID-19 Crisis Through a Migration Lens. Migration and Development Brief,* no. *32* (Washington: World Bank, 2020).

consequence, we can see how the meaning of security has been reduced to control, repression, surveillance, hiding the dimensions of care, protection and solidarity.

CONCLUSION: MOVING BEYOND RHETORIC OF CRISIS

This essay wants to draw attention to the risks of apostrophizing global political phenomena with sensational terminology such as *emergency* and *crisis*, which are tied to anxiety and fear about sudden and unexpected events, symptoms that can be easily fixed.

Migration, climate change and COVID-19 are not just *hic et nunc* crises, but political challenges that require structural changes to tackle these phenomena in a more comprehensive, long-term and holistic way.

As we have seen, there is a (hidden) link between the Pandemic, the infodemic—an excessive amount of information about a problem, which makes it difficult to identify a solution—and the phobocracy[37] that seems to still dominate the community and social holding of our country today. Which antidote to fear could we look for? How can we

145

---

37   Donatella Di Cesare, *Virus sovrano? L'asfissia capitalistica* (Torino: Bollati Boringhieri, 2020).

contrast the disinformation and politicization of these issues and go beyond the emergency narratives that contribute to fueling social anxiety, conflicts and the polarization in the public debate?

The EPC Report published in November 2020[38] shows that disinformation narratives about migration seek to exploit the readers' fears in order to polarize public opinion, manufacture discontent, sow divisions and set the political agenda. According to the EPC, disinformation actors link migration to existing insecurities, depicting it as a threat to three partially-overlapping areas: health, wealth and identity.

The Internet and social media have led to an explosion of all information sources—both truthful and false. The media usually show just a simplified and fragmented section of reality, not presenting the intertwined complexity behind phenomena such as migration, climate change and COVID-19. As insecurity is an excellent ground for the exercise of power, simplification and spectacularization led to a proliferation of fake news. Studies have shown that "falsehood diffused significantly farther, faster, deeper

38 https://wms.flexious.be/editor/plugins/imagemanager/content/2140/PDF/2020/Disinformation_on_Migration.pdf.

and more broadly than truth in all categories of information."[39] The rise of fake news has created a threatening and uncertain time for media communication and journalism. The spread of misinformation and dubious claims have led to a *post-truth* world, in which objective facts are less influential in shaping public opinion than appeals to personal belief and emotional logic. The current post-truth world is also characterized by multiple versions of one single fact and the rhetorical potential of communication, always available for manipulative purposes.

However, good and reliable information can save lives, build resilience, support livelihoods and empower people.[40] Information supply and investment on media literacy—learning how to distinguish reliable sources from fake news—should be prioritized in order to nurture people's critical thinking and reasoning. In phenomena such as migration, climate change and COVID-19, the media have the responsibility of unraveling fear and confusion and promoting emotional skepticism on issues. This isn't

---

39　Soroush Vosoughi, Deb Roy, and Sinan Aral, "The spread of true and false news online," *Science* 359, no. 6380 (2018): 1146.

40　Theodora Hannides, *Humanitarian Broadcasting in Emergencies: A Synthesis of Evaluation Findings*, Research Report, October 1, 2015 (London: BBC Media Action): 9.

just about funding more projects on news literacy, rather it is about teaching people to second-guess their instinctive reactions.

The political management of epidemics stages an idea of community, reveals the immune fantasies of a society and highlights the almighty dreams (and failures) of political sovereignty.[41] The combination of bio-political and sovereign powers result in, what Achille Mbembe[42] would call necropolitical regimes of power. The coronavirus is the spectacular expression of the planetary *impasse* in which humanity finds itself today.

Has this been a (missed) chance to shift media communication in the opposite direction? The current pandemic showed us how the biosphere and humankind are one, and how we are all part of a finite planet. Hence, we need to reconsider the concept of *hospitality*[43] as a priority and as the first ethical rule for our common humanity.[44] Rediscovering community— or rather the *in common*—is the only way to overcome fear.

148

41   Paul B. Preciado, "Learning from the virus," *ArtForum* (2020). https://www.artforum.com/print/202005/paul-b-preciado-82823.

42   Achille Mbembe, "The Universal Right to Breathe". *Critical Inquiry* (2020). https://critinq.wordpress.com/2020/04/13/the-universal-right-to-breathe/.

43   Jacques Derrida and Anne Dufourmantelle, *Sull'ospitalità* (Milano: Dalai, 2000).

44   Zygmunt Bauman, *Strangers at Our Door* (Cambridge: Polity Press, 2016).

*The links in the text were last accessed on 2 December 2020.

The ongoing pandemic calls for the seeing our lives as interdependent with others' (including viruses), their movements and, in general, their actions. As Mbembe points out:

> [Breathing] not only is it the right of every member of humankind, but of all life. It must therefore be understood as a fundamental right to existence. It is *an originary right to living* on Earth, a right that belongs to the universal community of earthly inhabitants, human and other.

Immune Co-habitation: Re-Framing Contagion Through Socio-Ecological Perspectives

Chiara Davino, Lorenza Villani and conversations with Serena Dambrosio and Marco Felicioni (Assembramenti) and with Piersandra Di Matteo

As mentioned in the previous chapters, immunity serves as the tangent point in which each body, be it individual or collective, human or non-human, encounters that which is different from it. Immunity has a compositional power able to make it a juncture between different entities, species and genders. In this sense, "if the semiotic axis around which every social institution is formed, is that which establishes the border between the self and the other—between us and them—nothing more than the principle of immunity can be both the key to its interpretation and the operational result."[1]

As we have seen, immunity can however take on an aggressive-military form which translates socially into a phobic fear of *contagion*, and spatially into the staging of ever new defensive barriers, both material and immaterial. The meaning, in the communal sense, of the concept of immunity, reverses the military semantics and leads to "[thinking] of it not so much as a discourse of invaders as of shared specificities in a semi-permeable self that is able to engage with

---

1   Roberto Esposito, *Immunitas. Protezione e negazione della vita* (Milano: Einaudi, 2002), 146.

others"[2] both human and non-human. This second communal dimension of immunity sees the body itself as an open system which, never given once and for all, is continuously defined by its relationship with the outside world. The immune system, seen as a border, therefore does not confine the body in a closed world, but instead structures itself as a permeable margin—although delicate and problematic—which organizes and manages the relationship with what is outside of the body itself, and what passes through it and changes it. In accordance with this perspective, rather than being a barrier of selection and exclusion for what is external and different, the immune system acts as an echo chamber for the other within the self which, dynamically, in turn, comes into being.[3]

Contrary to every aggressive-military interpretation tied to the concept of immunity, the immune system is in itself an alteration device, since every time it springs into action, it changes the body into something different from its previous state. In this sense, it is not the external body, the other,

2   Thyrza N. Goodeve, *Come una foglia. Thyrza Nichols Goodeve intervista Donna Haraway*, trans. Gina Maneri (Milano: La Tartaruga, 1999), 92–93. Original edition: Donna Haraway and Thyrza N. Goodeve, *How like a leaf* (London: Routledge, 1998).

3   Esposito, *Immunitas*, 166.

that is generating a change within the self, rather the immune system itself creating a new balance which overturns the incompatibility of the self's and the other's opposing forces, and makes them complementary.

In its widest sense, the immune system is not consequently the opposite of community, rather its completion, inasmuch as it is the filter that allows, as point of contact and interactive system between the self and the other, the very subsistence of the community and the self. This condition implies that the otherness is the very form that the self or the community take on when the internal encounters the external, or the own encounters the foreign.[4]

Within this framework, the body itself, be it individual or collective, becomes a place in which new alliances are formed, a space of constant *contamination*, which sees the world projecting itself within the body and thus defining it, in turn, as a different natural/cultural field.

In the first months of the SARS-CoV-2 pandemic, facing the intensification of the contagion containment measures and their more or less pronounced consequences took the form of global securitarian and exclusive

4   Ibid, 169.

rules, leading to the atomization of social relationships. Because of this, the authors, together with others, have attempted to profane the immune borders enforced by social distancing. The need to initiate a critical discussion on the various spatial implications triggered by the current historical events gave rise to Assembramenti in April 2020, during Italy's first lockdown. This is a collective made up of people who operate in the field of architecture, both academically and professionally, and which took shape in the digital space, in which the community met for the first time.

Assembramenti places itself along the immune borders to contrast social isolation and to attempt to challenge its mythologies, thereby reinterpreting the border itself as a space of alliance and contrast to its aggressive-military dynamics. Assembramenti has been an opportunity to instigate a change from a polarizing and oppositional immunity—which was then taking shape and has since strongly consolidated—to a common immunity, that of a subversive community of cultural sharing, in which 2020 and the Pandemic have been starting points for the deconstruction and reinterpretation of the contemporary social space on different scales, through different disciplines and diverse media.

In Assembramenti, the politicization of the space and the figures that investigate and design it, starts from the idea of (and the need for) a mutual contamination, among species, subjects, and disciplinary fields, to subvert the mythopoetic mechanisms of immunity that are instead based on the ontological incompatibility between self and other.

A community that is constantly evolving, which resists a specific form or output, Assembramenti inhabits the *onlife*, the hybrid existence in which the barrier between real and virtual, online and offline, has fallen. In this sense it is able to overturn the immune distances, turning them into a fertile ground for new alliances, new synergies between academic debate and design production, new narratives and visuals which reason on the pandemic space, on post-pandemic scenarios. More generally, on architecture as a cultural and procedural phenomenon, influenced by today's overlapping crises, but also as a *dimension* in which these crises manifest themselves and take shape, and, last but not least, as an instrument which mediates the relationships between people, and people and other species.

A first critical debate was incorporated into the volume *ZERO*, edited by Assembramenti, which contains textual and visual submissions by authors hailing from

different parts of the world.[5] As a whole,
these observations produce a narrative and
an unprecedented vision on the contemporary age and on the new ways to inhabit
the multitude of spaces in which we move
around daily.

From these observations, we have discussed with Serena Dambrosio (doctoral candidate in Architecture and Urban Studies at
the Pontificia Universidad Católica de Chile)
and Marco Felicioni (doctoral candidate in
History of Architecture at Università Iuav di
Venezia), members of the publishing group
of the project and co-founders of Assembramenti, together with Federico Bettazzi,
Michele Brusutti, Giovanni Casalini and the
authors of this volume.

5   Ed. Serena Dambrosio, Chiara Davino, Marco Felicioni, and Lorenza Villani,
     Assembramenti #ZERO (2021), https://assembramenti.net/wp-content/
     uploads/2021/04/ASSEMBRAMENTI-ZERO-Aprile-2021.pdf ; for an overview
     of the project: https://assembramenti.net/.

CONVERSATION WITH ASSEMBRAMENTI

Chiara Davino, Lorenza Villani: How was the project born and out of which necessities? The name itself, utilizing the term used at an institutional level to criminalize disorganized groups of people, was re-conceptualized to articulate a new critical community whose purpose is producing an alternative discussion to the contemporary immune one. What has Assembramenti ("public gatherings") meant over the years?

Serena Dambrosio: It all began in May 2020, when two dear friends invited me to a Zoom meeting. The idea was to open a discussion on the particular historical moment we were/are living, among people around the world who work somehow in the architectural field. The group did not have a name or a clear objective yet. This undefined and disordered dimension of the first meetings was precisely the reason that encouraged me to continue. I felt the need for spontaneous socialization, outside the patterns of order imposed on our lives by the Pandemic's containment measures. I soon realized that these encounters were restoring my curiosity about diversity and otherness, which confinement had taken away from my daily experience. Leaving aside the specific discussion on the relationship between the Pandemic and space, I believe that the desire to get to know people and experiences different from one's own in a relatively unpredictable context was the main driving force that allowed the group to evolve and survive. The choice to call this project Assembramenti has to do precisely with the claim of this need.

Marco Felicioni: Yes, exactly, as introduced by Serena, the name derives from the need to—literally—gather different minds. In Italian *assembrare* means "to gather" and *menti* means "minds." The project itself represents an immune reaction, a response to the prohibitions related to the health emergency. It brings about a need to socialize in a time when, physically, it is forbidden to be close to each other. Each of the participants, physically separated from the community, makes their contribution trying to interpret the moment we are living in their own way; they share their perception with others and claim their right to confront themselves. In Italy, "assembramenti" was the word of the year. One of those words no one had ever heard of until a few months ago, which now is on everyone's lips. During this emergency, the act of being together took on an inevitably negative connotation, at times criminal. Our project aimed exactly at preventing the idea that physical distancing must also imply

emotional distancing: we absolutely wanted
to avoid that.

Chiara Davino, Lorenza Villani: What does it mean
to act together when the social space has been
profoundly reconfigured? What shape do the
collective action and the alliance between
bodies in the digital meeting space take?
Serena Dambrosio: I would say that this alliance,
in our case, rather than a reconfiguration,
represents the condition of existence of this
community. Zoom calls, email exchanges,
Whatsapp groups, shared documents, Instagram posts, are the only spaces where this
community exists. Most of us don't know
each other in person. All our relationships are
mediated by the devices and platforms we use.
Marco Felicioni: Exactly, Assembramenti is a horizontal platform for a digital debate: through
the web and social media, it was transformed
into a collection of ideas that allowed us to
extend our network and to collect contributions from other people. This series of contributions has converged into the first issue of a
digital magazine: our ambition is to preserve
and re-propose this framework in the future,
even beyond this present emergency, in order
to interpret the new and eternal emergencies
that will arise from time to time.
Serena Dambrosio: Well, speaking about emergencies, I like to think that this project is

working like a virus within a virus: an entity that comes to life thanks to the possibilities of connection offered by the virtual space and taking advantage of the need for socialization caused by confinement. Probably, when the emergency is finally contained, the community will have to be rethought and reconfigured.

Marco Felicioni: I have a feeling that today, more than ever, collective action came to be a subversive action, having to face bans imposed either explicitly or implicitly. In this period, we can witness everyday groups of subversive gatherings fighting, in Hong Kong as well as in Minsk, to consolidate a still fragile and fictitious democracy. Similarly, sometimes one gets the impression that, even here in Europe, the society we live in can push us to isolate ourselves within our bubbles, discouraging constructive confrontation, leading us to passive acceptance. The pretext of physical distancing, during the Pandemic, has allowed us to greatly implement our digital sociality. And digital knowledge has allowed us, paradoxically, to broaden the range of our relationships: all of a sudden it was no longer necessary to live in the same city in order to spend time together. Digital tools existed well before, but their use was very different.

Chiara Davino, Lorenza Villani: What forms do the city, the urban and more generally the physical space take in the context of natural/cultural processes and the definitive consolidation of social processes, forms of sharing, and thought in the online space (intended as hybrid existence, devoid of barriers, between online and offline)?

Marco Felicioni: The city has exploded: it is a set of relationships, no longer related to physicality alone. Town planning, legislation and bureaucracy no longer keep up with the fast pace of technological development, which shortens any physical and geographical distance. Globalization causes the flapping of a butterfly's wings to trigger a hurricane on the other side of the planet. In an interconnected world, we cannot continue to think as individuals, disinterested in the problems of other countries, perhaps distant from us. As a matter of fact, a virus originated in a market in a Chinese city, and then caused a worldwide disaster. And a vaccine will be useless unless it is distributed equally to the entire world population. We need to find a model of sustainable development at a global level for the next challenges that await us, such as the climate emergency; it is unthinkable to deal with it in any other way than by taking action on a global level.

Serena Dambrosio: I would add that this extra-ordinary moment we are living is teaching us how dangerous the separation between spaces and processes could be for understanding the world around us. Physical space loses relevance when emptied of its activities and practices. At the same time, digital space cannot even be observed as abstracted from physical play. The existence of a virtual space necessarily implies the use of an enormous apparatus of material resources, the effects of which are often anything but ephemeral. Often the smart and sustainable rhetoric with which the digital products we buy are presented depends on a production system based on an extractivist and abusive logic of exploitation. For example, the production of lithium and copper, fundamental raw materials for the production of the technological devices we use every day, is linked to brutal extraction processes that are definitively compromising the functioning of the ecosystems and populations of vast areas of Latin America. All this makes an increasing need for a relational vision of the world to understand spaces and processes as indissolubly related categories evident.

Chiara Davino, Lorenza Villani: The different visualizations of the virus make heterogeneous spatialities emerge: of the environment, the body, the community, the public space, the inclusion and exclusion spaces, politics, media... What discussion has emerged through the open call? What was the spatiality which was mostly investigated as an urgent reflection?

Marco Felicioni: During the emergency new and unexpected spatialities were born. No one would ever have considered experiencing a concert from home, or attending international conferences directly from their living room, perhaps in slippers. The role of bodily physicality inevitably decreases, as it is no longer a necessary condition for our active social participation. The body is reduced to an undesirable means of transmission for the virus; better omit it in our relationship with others. As a result, the community is freed from the burden of spatial infrastructures: individuals seek to express themselves and reach each other through new communication channels. These are just some of the themes that emerged from the contributions collected through the Assembramenti call.

Serena Dambrosio: The general debate that emerged from this call confirms a public urgency to explore the relationship between spatial processes and new media, taking advantage of the pandemic context as a scenario in which this relationship reaches an extreme point. All the contributions investigate how virus visualization tools affect political decisions, acting spatially and socially; the consequences on subjective perceptions; the impacts on communities and collectivities; the relationship with specific visual rhetorics; the triggering of new dynamics of inclusion and exclusion—to name a few examples.

Marco Felicioni: Some contributors used Street View as a new tool for traveling, or Google Maps as a platform for digital drifts; others transformed their home garden into a stage for performances; others reflected on the domesticization of the workspace, on how the virus camouflaged the city through new anti-contagion scenographies, or invited us to pause and look in a new way at roads that we have always walked casually.

Serena Dambrosio: We believe that each contribution proposes, each in its own way, a different possibility to interpret and critically visualize spatial transformations related to the processes we are experiencing on a global and national level. We consider that in Italy these discussions are absolutely absent. For this reason, we decided to carry out the project exclusively in Italian. In this way, we hope to give a modest contribution so that new networks of discussions and questions can be opened to deeply investigate the transformations we are experiencing starting from common cultural geography.

Chiara Davino, Lorenza Villani: Going back to the heterogeneous spatial realities: the interscalarity of the virus, from the body to the planet, can be read as an occasion to rethink architecture beyond the mostly operative and normative aspects with which it is often interpreted in Italy, favoring a more interdisciplinary, cultural and political, inclusive role. Could this happen?

Serena Dambrosio: I fully agree with this view and I would say that it is not only a possible but above all a necessary opportunity. I believe that in recent times we are rediscovering a new communicative dimension of architecture, as an agent of visualization of political, social, environmental and cultural processes, historically excluded from conversations considered strictly inherent to disciplinary concerns. In my opinion, this communicative dimension may represent a first step towards rethinking architecture more in terms of relationships than of objects. I consider Assembramenti as part of this intention: to highlight the complex network of relationships that interact in the material and symbolic construction of the spatial processes in which we situate ourselves as individuals but above all as a community.

Marco Felicioni: Absolutely, as mentioned above, the operational and regulatory aspects related to architecture are no longer able to keep up with the speed of changes affecting today's world. Never more than now is it urgent to reconsider and expand our conception of this discipline. The virus is invisible, but its effects are macroscopic; it triggers processes that affect every area of society. This interscalarity is the greatest lesson that architecture can draw from the Pandemic: only by reasoning in holistic, interdisciplinary terms and by designing processes over time, can it really return to affect the changes in the world.

Chiara Davino, Lorenza Villani: The contemporary immune mythologies outline socio-spatial risk zones in which the otherness is marginalized, criminalized and spatially separated. What political role does then the architect, or the Assembramenti project in general, take in the deconstruction of these mythologies?
Serena Dambrosio: Following on from the previous answer, I think that the architect's political role in deconstructing these mythologies is precisely to make them appear as such: make the relation between ideological structures and material world evident; visualize the points of encounter and clash between design practice as the superimposition of a subjective intention on a plural and heterogeneous reality; highlighting how the socio-spatial limits that these mytholo-

gies imply are abstract and arbitrary; on the other hand highlighting how the territories in which we move and operate are fluid and continuous. I believe that our role is to make it clear that the material reality in which we live is only one of the possible realities. Assembramenti, in my opinion, contributes to this objective.

Marco Felicioni: Exactly, I believe that the key lies in giving priority to bottom-up processes; in pointing out and denouncing every form of latent spatial imposition, and working for its abatement. Isolation increases social inequalities and the state of emergency justi-fies previous forms of inequality. Only an inclusive design will offer fair and valid alternatives to the present, as well as a possible future for everyone. Assembramenti works exactly in this direction: it seeks to bring back attention toward urgent global issues at a local level, by expressing them in the Italian language; it makes a new and enlarged public aware; it re-launches and extends the consideration of an architect's work in the contemporary world.

DWELLING

The overcoming of the paradigm of immunity in aggressive-military terms in favor of one of community translates into *forms of dwelling* structured on the de-estrangement between humans and between humans and non-humans, and on the establishment of new kinships between species and bodies, at the bottom of which is an interconnection of responsibilities. The latter was meant by Donna Haraway as the imperative to question the repercussions of our actions and who we are responsible for.[6] In this sense, existence in the world is not reduced to the simple presence in some place, but is tied to the concept of *taking care* of the subjects/objects which constitute it. Taking care, which is the fundamental trait of dwelling according to Heidegger, implies the de-estrangement between humans and the environment, so that both, in a mutual relationship that is not instrumental, can enjoy their own existence.[7] This condition displaces humanity from its uncontested overlordship

---

6 Donna J. Haraway, *Chthulucene. Sopravvivere su un pianeta infetto*, trans. Claudia Durastanti and Clara Ciccioni (Roma: Not, 2019), 14–15. Original edition: *Staying with the Trouble. Making Kin in the Chthulucene* (Chicago: University of Chicago Press, 2016).

7 Mimmo Pesare, *Abitare ed esistenza. Paideia dello spazio antropologico* (Milano: Mimesis Edizioni, 2009), 59–97.

of the world, in favor of a form of dwelling revolving around *living among things*, namely the care one has of things for the time we *inhabit* them. A form of "dwelling" which allows different species to create *kinships* among themselves, meant as alliances which create *companions,* in terms of the various earthly connections which exist among them and that do not require human exceptionalism.[8]

This form of dwelling, which gives each species a form of agency, of performativity and a projectuality is compromised by the capitalist dynamics of consumption which have characterized the last two centuries, and more. In this sense the very term "Anthropocene" according to some critics, among which Donna Haraway, is but a way to emphasize the typical anthropocentrism of the human perspective, putting a generic *anthropos* at the center of the scene, hiding the responsibilities of capitalist development, the true driving force of the ongoing environmental catastrophe. Anthropocene's anthropocentrism, however, backfires insofar as the human action is re-introduced in a complex system of actions which cannot

8 Haraway, *Chthulucene*, 28.

be attributed to a single agent, rather to a chain of agencies. In this regard, as soon as the human approaches non-human beings, he does not find them inert, which would allow him to think himself a lone actor. On the contrary, he finds in them an agency that is strictly tied to human action. It is in this sense that the natural and the social are indistinguishable as both are part of complex blends and connections.[9]

Contemporary crises evidently show these *socio-ecological* relationships through concatenations that link the global to the local and amplify their range. For example, "without destabilized natural habitats, intensive capitalist agriculture, dispossessed local communities driven deeper into the hinterland, uncontrolled urbanization, or globalized logistics networks it's hard to imagine corona having this widespread of an impact."[10]

The closing of national borders, the intensification of securitarian politics and military logics have therefore to be interpreted as the effect of a larger anthropogenic process, the fractures of which are generated

170

9   Bruno Latour, *La sfida di Gaia. Il nuovo regime climatico*, trans. Donatella Caristina (Milano: Meltemi, 202), 101–102. Original edition: *Face à Gaïa. Huit conférences sur le nouveau régime climatique* (Paris: La Découverte, 2015).

10   Salar Mohandesi, "Crisis of a new type," *Viewpoint Magazine* (May 13, 2020): par. 62.

and perpetuate one another. In this regard there is no global solution, but only local experiments which open new scenarios on how to inhabit the Earth in a system of new kinships among different species.

The responsibility of the architectural and urban disciplines, in the context described up until this point, involves the ability to convey an idea of space which will always take into consideration broad geographies and multiple subjects, beyond the restricted geometries *to be designed*. Through these spatial and projectual understandings, which imply socio-ecological relationships on a broader scale, it is possible to redraft, by going back to Lefebvre's thought, a new "right to the city."[11] The city is understood not as an urban conglomerate, but rather as a political entity in which every subject dwells, and as a space in which actions do not terminate within the strictly urban borders. In this sense, the right to the city configures itself as re-appropriation, by humans and non-humans, deprived of their agency space, of the very projectual and creative capacity so that the space itself becomes the drawing of the intercon-

---

11 Henri Lefebvre, *Le droit à la ville* (Paris: Éditions Anthropos, 1968).

nections and the agencies of the subjects which dwell in it and cross it. Even today the right to the city configures itself—albeit in different terms, as new spatialities and new subjects are involved—as a critique to urbanization that polarizes and creates peripheries both in social and spatial terms.

In such a system, the activation of *other* practices within urban and non-urban spaces, takes on a fundamental role. These spaces rehabilitate the different subjects, reconnecting them to the others and generating new forms of kinship based on responsibility and care.

The practice of dwelling built on the idea of a common immunity thus acts by contrasting the processes of an immune system which acts in aggressive-military terms and manifests itself also through the process of making certain subjects invisible. These subjects, deemed potential threats, are excluded and marginalized through the large body of architectures, debates and laws of the mythological machine. If before COVID-19 the forms of precariousness and de-legalization which stem from the violence enacted along the borders fell directly on the *undesirable* bodies of those who attempted to cross the borders, it is only during the Pandemic that the conditions of the migratory processes have worsened, following the absurd equation *migration equals virus*. To this effect the *war on the virus* has intensified, and legitimized, the *war on the migrant*, further hindering the possibility of entry in the countries of the north of the world. In the pandemic context, which has highlighted the different levels of vulnerability and im-mobility which structure our societies, the triennial European cooperation project Atlas of Transition – New Geographies for a Cross-Cultural Europe, active since 2017 in Italy, Albania, Belgium, Poland, France, Greece and Sweden, has confirmed the necessity to carry on the already-begun discourse on the right to the city and social appearance.

The conversation with Piersandra Di Matteo (performing arts theorist, dramaturg, curator, research fellow at the Università Iuav di Venezia and artistic director of Atlas of Transition) allows one to dig deeper into the project, aimed at encouraging the intercultural dialog between European citizens and new arrivals, through the performative arts. Indeed Atlas of Transition looks to the possibilities stemming from the migratory phenomenon of today, contrasting the hostility with which it is on the other hand perceived within society, through an open and communal study on the new shared ways of living the public space.

The different projects which make up Atlas of Transition have re-activated, throughout the years, urban spaces giving them new meanings, and have built thanks to performance practices and the socio-spatial redrawing of the urban fabric, new connections between those who inhabit the city.

The string of anti-COVID measures that were enacted in 2020 have strongly reduced part of the project, reframing it on the digital platform International Summer School Performing Resistance, aimed at sparking a debate between academics, activists, artists, performers and a vast international audience on the subversive and resistance-related role of the performance practices. It is during the COVID-19 pandemic, which consolidated social borders, inequalities and existing conflicts, that the very impossibility of instigating performance practices has further defined the essential condemning role against increasingly solid dynamics of *social invisibilization*.

CONVERSATION WITH PIERSANDRA DI MATTEO

Chiara Davino, Lorenza Villani: How have the uncertainty and precarity caused by the COVID-19 pandemic been transformed into a different working method? In the name of this year's edition, *resistance* takes the shape of an active methodology, indispensable to counter the deep and structural emergency-related crises of today's social organization.

Piersandra Di Matteo: The peculiarity of the curatorial practices lies in their ability to promote a *poetics of relations*, producing new contexts, articulating new modes of perception, promoting a collective discursive space, questioning forms of representation, spatiality and temporality that concern a redistribution and the fabric of our social bodies, inventing new ecosystems. In curating Atlas of Transitions Biennale, we encouraged unexpected dynamics between inhabitants and the urban environment, enacting spatial intensities in practices of everyday life, open to an ethical demand for diversity, that exceeds categories of identifiable difference, contrasting that hybrid space *in-between* where the *thought of self* and the *thought of the other* become obsolete in their duality. This Biennale was promoted by Emilia Romagna Teatro Fondazione (Emilia

Romagna Theatre Foundation) in the frame of Creative Europe, a large-scale project conceived to deal with contemporary migration from an artistic perspective, encouraging interchanging geographies based on reciprocity and interaction. With the festivals entitled Right to The City (2018) and Home (2019) we decided to suspend the *habitus* of performance programming and act concretely, developing a network with various urban institutions including the Museum of Contemporary Art, the Cinematheque and the Foundation for Urban Innovation, the Academy of Fine Arts, the Women's Italian Library; non-governmental organizations such as Amnesty International and Mediterranea Saving Humans, a migrant rescue ship saving people in the Mediterranean sea... Programming participatory projects, workshops, concerts, screenings and informal encounters did not take shape before coming into resonance with the activities, living conditions and urgencies that are part of the lives of migrants in Reception Centres, in a continuous dialogue with the cultural and social cooperatives involved in migrant hospitality and social care, promoting persistent actions in the outskirts of the city—avoiding a gentrification of audiences aimed at shifting, superficially perhaps, groups of people from the centre to the outskirts, but in such a way as to experience these areas and mix spectators and levels of language. We also involved independent theatres, associations of immigrant communities, the Centre for Women Against Violence, high school and university students, activists, and many others. This dense network of connections allowed contexts, languages and instances of desiring to intermingle, bringing different spectators together in a productive system of concatenations. We worked to promote corporeal posture and participatory projects to create polyrhythmic fields of interaction that could identify interferences, dissonances and elements of discontinuity in *urban life*, in order to reveal its internal areas of friction, conflict and opacity. We wished to set out reciprocal areas of collaboration between citizens, inhabitants, immigrants and newcomers, countering any rationale of racial, sexual, cultural, economic subordination: ways to reappropriate public space, breaking the apparatus of routine through which singularities are controlled and disciplined. The result of this sort of re-appropriation inevitably depends upon the exercise of collective power to reshape processes of urbanization and the daily experience of the subjects, by creating a qualitatively different kind of urban sociality, counter-blasting abstract spatial models as an agency of transformation that affects social models, cultural conventions and personal coefficients. In only a few months, the hurricane-like impact of the Pandemic forced us to face radical changes. Any thought concerning this can only begin with the awareness that—as Judith Butler affirms—the virus can strike anyone, while the management of the crisis reinforces the system of capitalist exploitation with radical inequality and other forms of heteropatriarchal violence: digging trenches for the precarization of forms of life. The bodily closeness necessary for our activities, their collective dimension and inclusive participation all received a moral blow from the anti-COVID measures. The festival scheduled for June 2020 was canceled and part of it became an autonomous project that took its own renewed form in the International Summer School Performing Resistance, a digital discursive platform aimed at exploring the ways in which artistic practices build spaces of resistance, forms of subversion, counter-hegemonic postures on migration, actions capable of outlining other visions of and in contemporary cities. Originally, the Summer School was conceived for 30 participants selected through a public call. The response and interest were extraordinary:

more than 130 people from Cuba to Afghanistan, from Brazil to Mexico submitted their candidacies. So, due to the COVID situation, we decided to reverse the plan and therefore reformulate an online and open dimension, a series of Dialogues on the Arts, Migrations, Inclusive Cities: an occasion for scholars, activists, curators and international artists to discuss and explore together issues such as the borderline between art and activism, the creation of alternative *system* of knowledge countering silenced and invisibilized subjectivities, the notion of participation, the right to the city, critically reflecting on borders and mobility. For example, Lilie Chouliaraki investigated the processes of symbolic representation of the *victims* in the Pandemic, focusing on a detailed analysis of populist rhetoric; from another perspective, Nikos Papastergiadis offered a reflection on the future scenarios of public art and its key role in sharing imaginaries and collaborative practices in the post-pandemic; Marco Martiniello, director of the Center for Ethnic and Migration Studies at the University of Liège, turned his attention to the *post-racial* generation that manifests itself in urban space through locally rooted but interconnected artistic collaborative practices at a transnational level; Sandro Mezzadra and Michael Hardt discussed the experience of Mediterranea Saving Humans, of which they are both promoters, a starting point for crucial issues concerning current migration policy: from the mutations of humanitarianism to the crisis of human rights, from freedom of movement to the autonomy of migration. The Finnish-Nigerian journalist Minna Salami discussed the notion of "afropolitanism" and the need to activate a *sensuous*, and feminist, *knowledge* capable of inaugurating decolonial and anti-racist approaches. Daniel Blanga Gubbay analysed educational projects conceived within the artistic institution capable of producing spaces and methods of transmission for invisibilized knowledge. Moving from urban centers to the periphery of Europe, Federica Mazzara examined the strategies implemented by artists to challenge the narratives that negatively stigmatize migrants, focusing in particular on the issue of deaths at sea; Karina Horsti offered a critical reflection on how cultural institutions and operators, artists and activists can make invisible borders visible, analyzing the resulting consequences. And more... After the Summer School, in the winter (2-7 December 2020)—making a big effort in programming—we presented the final Biennale festival, We The People—an edition of course marked by the limitations imposed by the Pandemic. We didn't believe in the dictatorship of the *show must go on* nor simply adapt to the repercussions of the current change of paradigm. We wanted to invent a space to remain alert and take note of fault lines and trenches, raise defenses against inequalities that become normalized in the blink of an eye. We also didn't want to neglect safeguarding artistic work on an aesthetic level and artists as workers. So we put together a program of film projections, radiophonic incursions, workshops for high-school students, assemblages of archived sounds from a non-Eurocentric perspective, interwoven vocal gestures sent by dozens of citizens, concerted acts of silence, exchanges of sound heritages among women with different origins. Each action sets out, in its own way, an encounter within an *acoustic space*. This was above all a question of creating relations involving closeness at a distance, weaving together sources, making room for noncompliant postures. Each action foreseen provided a chance to *act in concert*. This was not an invitation to move towards conformity, but to negotiate convergent/divergent aims capable of countering racial, gender-based, social and economic subalternity. We The People, the final edition of Atlas of Transitions Biennale, thus decided to exist, and did so by deploying a micropolitics of listening. The spectator, here, was above all someone who opens themselves to listening, and who pays attention to voices that are ignored or silenced, singular or collective pronunciations. The materiality of a listening that contemplates loss and extreme presence, the energy of informal interactions, the strength of voices, tremors and noises, donated verses, the rhythms of narrations linked to unrecognized rights: all of this cuts across, in various ways, the cluster of actions making up the festival. This acoustic theatre is an agonistic space, made of relational poetics that decenter whiteness, heterosexuality and affective inadequacies. In listening, we encounter one another as bodies, bodies that come together in an assemblage that, in its existence here and now, is already headed towards something else; towards another act of listening.

Chiara Davino, Lorenza Villani: How can we imagine the role of the performing arts as practices of resisting the processes of immunisation, invisibilization and exclusion at a time when being present together and appearing in physical public space is forbidden, limited or shifted into the digital dimension?

Piersandra Di Matteo: Our days of quarantine were characterized by a fundamental affection: a yearning for bodies. It was a movement that flowed with varying intensity, an emotional state that affects not just human bodies, but all bodies equally: animal, plant, mineral, matter of any form. The action of physical bodies—the core of the performing arts—was then impaired and threatened by an exhaustion that comes from simply waiting for a return to normality. "We will not return to normality" not only "because normality was the problem," as the members of the Delight Lab Collective shouted from Santiago de Chile during the confinement, but also because of the truth behind what Paul B. Preciado said: "You cannot go back to a normal life, because what you used to call 'normal life' cannot exist during a shift of paradigm, because even if things always seem the same, they no longer are. Even words that seem pronounced the same way have a different sense. The problem is that no one knows what their new meaning will be. Will it be decided by an algorithm? Will it be announced on Instagram? Or will it be introduced by a legislative decree? You will return with your bags full of words and things, only to realise that you don't have the right definitions." How can we question our words, to avoid using them without grasping their changed meaning? Words such as "inclusion," "participation," "closeness?" How can artistic practices and politics, ecological perspective reinvent and affirm once again the power of bodies? What has become of those bodies? What forms does *liveness* take on under social distancing? But also; how is it possible to go onstage and ensure safety for workers in the performing arts? And spectators? What are the material and economic conditions of our work? In Italy, our sector is undergoing a severe crisis: 70% of workers in the performing arts are unemployed... In Italy, the ones who have reopened are mainly the large institutions, the national theatres who can guarantee they will cover expenses for maintaining hygiene. But what about smaller groups? The ones who truly represent the creative and innovative fabric now found... What will happen to the ones who work locally, in contact with citizens? It is clear that the measures being adopted and to be adopted in the next few months will lead to cuts in production, a tendency to move towards performances with monologues or only a few actors onstage, for practical reasons. The number of spectators is also dropping. And so are tours, as well as the chance for encounters and exchanges and—even worse—there will be a fall in the attention given to the African, Arab and Middle

Eastern scenes, which had made considerable growth in recent years. This contraction will be legitimated by the impossibility of travelling, quarantines when entering or leaving a country, laws for prevention introduced by each country... This is an extremely serious question, which will have to be monitored carefully, so as not to all back into confirmative and Eurocentric, or with the term used by Minna Salami, "Europatriarchal" curating practices. After the lockdown, some contemporary theatre festivals in Italy have tried to re-open, in public spaces, with a small number of spectators. There's something about these experiences that can be called *acts of resistance*. On this occasion I had a very strong feeling: something related to the question of quantity. It's about numbers, the rush to sell out performances, a way of thinking that considers a festival to be a success based on the amount of people present, how events are organised and tickets handed out: all of this data must be handed over to local authorities, governments and European bodies, to make sure the funding arrives. This way of thinking, based on numbers, has been reinforced over time, and is now considered normal or even essential, a fact, with no critical reflection. Now the Pandemic is definitely teaching us to reconsider this muscular performativity of numbers. It's not a question of favouring a niche, or the privileged few but of using curating as a cure, close to communities, local areas, working with *contact* as a practice in the era of social distancing... We should encourage encounters in which it truly is possible to face one another. But the most critical aspect of this fall in numbers is: who is left out? How to ensure that the movement of inclusive practices and actions, linked to long-term processes in local areas, is not sacrificed in this *cure of the little*? So the performing arts have an important function in promoting a poetics of relations that leaves no one behind. This has consequences for our way of conceiving curation... What we need is a new way of thinking, something that can come by working together: something that is urgently required, new paradigms...

Chiara Davino, Lorenza Villani: Over the last year, a series of protests in Italy and worldwide have drawn new attention to the centrality of the body as a political space; at the same time, many virtual gatherings have been formed, understood as forms of resistance with their own timing, modalities and physicality. What does this split situation imply for *action*?

Piersandra Di Matteo: The antiracist uprisings of the Black Lives Matter movement in the

United States, in the wake of the murder of George Floyd, which rapidly spread to other areas of the world, including Italy, gave way to new interracial, intersectional and intergenerational coalitions. A new energy flowed into public space. The multiracial nature of these mobilizations and protests, which put some amount of strain on the racist social pact on which American democracy is founded, gained momentum and became more widespread in the name of social rights and justice, plunging its roots into a ground that had been prepared by years of struggles and discourses. This alliance among bodies imposed itself on public space, affirming collective action: here, the body is a tool for politics, the foundation of a *people in action* that speaks on behalf of subjects struggling together and acting in concert. A powerful alliance of bodies was behind the performance piece *Un violador en tu camino*, conceived by the Chilean feminist collective Las Tesis: thousands of Chilean women occupied public arenas to demonstrate, with their own bodies and their own voices, against rape and unpunished violence against women, and thus condemn, with a demonstrative act, Chile's patriarchal system. This flash mob went viral and turned into a transfeminist *tide* that swept across the world, reaching as far as India. Digital technology unquestionably contributed to sharing, spreading and organizing these protests. What is at stake in digital space is a very serious matter. Digital technologies and IT skills are no doubt ambivalent tools, and I believe they must be considered as an arena for struggle and conquest. The acceleration of digitalization processes, which have swept into employment and services, and the exponential growth of platform capitalism, made clear during the months of the Pandemic forms of exploitation of labor and new strategies of surveillance promoted by the new securitarian politics. Digital technology draws a line between those who have access to the web and data, and those who are excluded. Being tempted by technological Luddism is useless. I believe it is essential to grasp the web's counter-hegemonic potential, be it through organizing forms of mutualism, cooperative self-organization or practices involving care for collective life. One might recall the digital assemblies that worked towards creating collective infrastructures and commoning processes. Or again, the online dynamics that enable processes of bodily proximity, or connections on various scales (local, national, European) to program and organize a reappropriation of urban space and public occupation.

Chiara Davino, Lorenza Villani: Immunitarian mythologies make spatial borders and processes of confinement ubiquitous. What might be a starting point for the responsibility of the visual and performing arts in deconstructing these borders?

Piersandra Di Matteo: During the Pandemic our bodies have become repressed as a consequence of the lockdown, disarmed by enforced confinement and numbed by individualized recriminations and by biomedical measures. We are experiencing a whole series of restrictions to our most basic freedoms, all in the name of public health and safety. The issue of borders, confinement, forms of self-reclusion, as well as the bodily diffidence introduced in daily life and legitimated by the diktat of *social distancing*, are all elements that we cannot ignore in the immediate present and in the years to come. As is well known, borders progressively took on a specific political significance in European modernity, marking—through their representation as lines on maps—the territory of a State, endorsing and facilitating colonial expansion. In their book *Border as a Method*, Sandro Mezzadra and Brett Neilson show how, in our time, a certain number of global processes have questioned this consolidated representation of borders, transforming no other than borders into places of intense and often lethal conflict. Control over mobility, in particular, is at the heart of these conflicts, in which other definitions of the border become central once again, definitions involving race, gender, society, language, culture, the body, etc. Today, one must also add the borders sanctioned by the rationale of immunity. In the case of migrations, while those driven to cross borders do so in search of freedom and equality, restricting or denying this possibility is aimed at reproducing inequality in the freedom of movement and reintroducing the original link between frontiers and violence. I believe that art plays an essential role in exposing this link. I might answer your question better by referring to *Necropolis*, by Byelorussian artist Arkadi Zaides, a performance we presented as an event in Atlas of Transitions Biennale. The project stems from a reading of a document drafted by UNITED for Intercultural Action, which lists the more than forty thousand migrants who died trying to reach Europe between 1993 and 2020, many without a name or indication of their burial place. The choreographer and a group of collaborators invented a methodology to reconstruct these absences and make them worthy of mourning. They searched through databases, archives and municipal, cemetery and hospital authorities, locating places, geolocating them, visiting these places and documenting the moment of their visit through a shot from their point of view. Using Google Earth, *Necropolis* gives us a virtual map of the dead: it uses the cartography tool, that is, to reconstruct the real map of invisible bodies. The visits to graves and burial places were, in any case, ways to visualize the data found on the list, through a process of embodiment. *Necropolis* relates the macro-scale of Google Earth to the micro-scale of skin surfaces. This performance, not by chance, pits the coldness of the data against the visceral impact of the cadaveric, the flesh, the decomposition of the body (in the second part): the sculptural presence of a body in an advanced state of decay comes across like an appeal to forensic medicine, that has stopped working on recognizing the corpses. Concretely speaking, *Necropolis* challenges the concept of the border, which is not only the sea—the geographical one— but also involves the death of migrants in the various urban contexts visited by the project in the heart of Europe. These are subjects who carry the border within themselves, in their transits: in the reception centers and at the French-Italian border, while their silenced death is given a new presence, a presence that defines a world of violence.

REFLECTIONS ON
DE-BORDERING PRACTICES

The role of artistic practices in defining new ways to perceive public spaces, at the same time studying the relationship between the aesthetic dimension and politics, and the ways through which the performances relate to the space, allows therefore the overcoming of the processes of *bordering* that turn ever more frequently the biological body in a first form of boundary toward the other. The body becomes a border which, through its ways of acting and dwelling, strengthens the geographical borders. Along these borders, the narrations of national security (such as the fight against human trafficking or terrorism) and the building of an emotional scenario based on fear and insecurity justify, on one side, the forms of militarization of borders, and on the other, the perpetuation of colonial logics of exclusion.[12]

Thus the institutional representations of borders, and the immune geographies of polarization and im-mobility are juxtaposed with

---

12   See Maurizio Albahari, *Crimes of Peace: Mediterranean Migrations at the World's Deadliest Border* (Philadelphia: Penn Publishing Company, 2015) ; Pierluigi Musarò, "Mare Nostrum: the visual politics of a military-humanitarian operation in the Mediterranean Sea," *Media, Culture & Society* 39, no. 1 (2017): 11-28 ; Gaia Giuliani, "Il mostro che viene dal sud del mondo," *Jacobin Italia* 6, (2020): 38-43.

the known forms of action, or counter-narratives, which render visible what the mythological machine either omits or trivializes.

The *de-bordering* process of the ways in which borders are narrated and represented, in their interpretations be they physical, symbolic or in the media, together with a de-bordering of the responsibility spaces through creative and communal actions, are the key points of numerous performance and visual projects that we have encountered in recent years. Communal counter-narratives, as is the case of *Referendum* by Cuban visual artist and activist Tania Bruguera[13] and *Remembering Lampedusa* by Finnish media and migrations scholar Karina Horsti.[14]

In the first case, through the second edition of Atlas of Transition, Home (2019), the performance has activated a campaign of urban referendum directed at the citizens of Bologna, Italy, inviting them to express their opinion on the issue "borders kill, should we abolish borders?". Numerous practices, among which urban bulletin boards, emplacements in theaters, cultural centers

---

13   See https://bologna.emiliaromagnateatro.com/spettacolo/tania-bruguera-referendum-2/.
14   See https://rememberinglampedusa.com/ ; Karina Horsti and Klaus Neumann, "Memorializing mass deaths at the border: two cases from Canberra (Australia) and Lampedusa (Italy)," *Ethnic and Racial Studies* 42, no. 2 (2019): 141-158.

and social clubs, leafleting and public interventions, have contributed to the definition of the project in which the formation of volunteers which have manned the polling stations has helped in the arguing of the artistic choices and promoting an open dialog with the passers-by on the issue of borders in daily life.

Conversely, the research project and collaborative film *Remembering Lampedusa* (2019) revolves around the assertion of memory, otherwise invisible, of the October 3, 2013 shipwreck of a craft full of migrants, primarily from Eritrea, close to Lampedusa—after which the Italian government launched the Mare Nostrum military and humanitarian mission in the central Mediterranean. This project contains the accounts of the survivors and the victims' relatives, but also of citizens of Lampedusa who helped in the rescue and relief after the incident, as an active part of the creative process. The anonymity and normalization of death along the European borders are juxtaposed to firsthand memories, emotions and considerations, in an inclusive process for a more welcoming society. To the shaping of borders which make those who cross them illegal, concentrating on their attempt in terms of risks, breach of the law and restrictions, the artistic prac tices juxtapose human aspects and abilities of reflection otherwise *impossible* in a society based on immunization.

FROM VIOLENCE TO THE NATURAL CONTRACT

In Goya's *Fight with Cudgels*, the artist portrays two duelists trapped knee-deep in a quagmire of mud. After every movement, they sink deeper into the swamp in which they are fighting, until they bury each other: their sinking is thus proportional to the aggressiveness of their fight.

This image shows two wars, one subjective between the two duelists, and one objective that pits the two enemies, unknowingly paired, against the objective world in which they are fighting. The first form of violence, subjective, is represented by classical wars, in which peoples clash with other peoples more or less indiscriminately and visibly. This form of violence, which evidently emerges in the militarization of borders, has its origin in the very social contract whose primeval aim it is to prevent the continuation of violence, which would otherwise continue forever. In this sense, through the social contract, every individual, having abandoned its natural state, makes an alliance which leads to more security.[15] However, this form of alliance, by organizing society, produces groups of a different nature which, as stated previously, are increasingly polarized with regard to access to resources, dignity and rights. Some of these groups—precarious transnational nomads, refugees or migrants, asylum seekers or illegal aliens—create a disturbance in the imagery of contemporary societies, and for this, as if their lives were worthless, they become illegal and lose their rights.[16]

Subjective war is supplemented by objective violence which, going back to Goya's painting, involves a third element, the quagmire; it is very likely that the earth itself, breaking in, will devour the two fighters before they have resolved their differences. This third party, today reduced to a scenario, is an active subject on which the effects of the actions of the two duelists act and react. In short, every action ends up exercising

15 Jean Jacques Rousseau, *Il contratto sociale*, trans. Valentino Gerratana (Torino: Einaudi, 1977), 23–25. Original edition: *Du contrat social: ou principes du droit politique* (Amsterdam: Marc Michel Rey, 1762).

16 One can think about how the term "refugee" is often used interchangeably with the term "migrant". The latter is utilized to negate the legitimacy of the request for protection, while the former indicates and highlights the good reasons for the presence of the person and such a request. See Didier Fassin, *Le vite ineguali. Quanto vale un essere umano*, trans. Lorenzo Alunni (Milano: Feltrinelli, 2019), 60. Original edition: *La vie. Mode d'emploi critique* (Paris: Seuil, 2018).

violence not only on the humans, but also on the non-humans involved. As it is argued in the previous paragraphs, this third party seen by humans as little more than a stage for their exploits, is formed by infinite subjects/objects which, each with their own agency, their own projectuality and performativity, co-belong to the world alongside humans.

In the drawing up of this contract, which Serres calls "natural," the relationship that the human has with the non-human would cease to be one of dominion and ownership, but one of reciprocity, symbiosis and respect; knowledge would not assume ownership, nor action assume dominion. A contract at the base of which is the right of symbiosis which is defined by the reciprocity between nature and humans; in fact, as much as nature gives unto humans, the latter should give back to the former, now having become a subject of rights.[17]

It is this very contract that, according to Serres, is the first quasi-object, inasmuch it is able to make relationships concrete and put together nature and society, or even better, reconfigure them as a single entity.

---

17 Michel Serres, *Il contratto naturale,* trans. Alessandro Serra (Milano: Feltrinelli, 1991), 59–60. Original edition: *Le contrat naturel* (Paris: Éditions François Bourin, 1990).

This co-belonging to the world requires a flexible system of restrictions, responsibilities and freedoms, which, although without language, is able to relay information to each of the elements attached to it, about them and the system itself, thus giving them confidence and creating new kinships.

The *inclusive* redefinition of the idea of space, and therefore the ability to understand it as a product of new alliances and kinships between humans and non-humans, allows for an understanding of every process taking place in a socio-ecological perspective, able to keep together several processes that are apparently very distant. This perspective gives therefore new insights and new spatial awarenesses which, we believe, are necessary to redefine the very idea of space, and more generally, of architecture.

The investigation on today's immune morphologies, through a reading of the concatenation of anthropic, ecological and social processes, allows us to define the social and complex role of the architectural and urban disciplines, more generally of the spatial and social practices, the primary responsibility of which is, for us, to convey an idea of space as a healing process in which everyone's action, manifesting itself on a local and global scale, shows the responsibilities of our shared co-existing in the world.

BIOGRAPHIES

Malvina Borgherini, associated professor, is scientific director of MeLa Media Lab and ClusterLAB *LSD Public Imaginaries, Forms of Displaying* at Università Iuav di Venezia, where she teaches at Master Degree in Architecture, at Bachelor Degree in Multimedia Arts and at Master Degree in Theater and Performatives Arts. At Iuav she is also director of the Postgraduate Program MOVIES Moving Images Arts. In the last decade her research activity has focused on the new languages of contemporary, looking with great attention to the images and their capacity to create new forms of spatiality and expression within urban communities. Convinced that the images are not only the result of an authorial production, but also the reflection of social and political events that characterizes contemporary urban communities, with the MeLa Media Lab she participated as scientific director in a series of international projects.

Serena Dambrosio is a doctoral candidate in Architecture and Urban Studies at Pontificia Universidad Católica de Chile. She's interested in architecture as a cultural phenomenon, investigated through media and representation techniques as discursive tools. She has been a doctoral student fellow at the Canadian Center for Architecture (2019) and visiting research fellow at the Het Nieuwe Instituut (2020). She is the author of different kinds of publications related to her research field. She also participates in self-organized groups of researchers, students, teachers, architects, and artists to question conventional spaces of learning in art and architecture including Assembramenti, La escuela nunca, Porunhabitardigno.

Chiara Davino is an architect, researcher and PhD candidate in Sociology and Social Reaserch at the Sociology and Business Law Department Università di Bologna, and co-founder of the platform Assembramenti. She studied at Universidade Autonoma de Lisboa and graduated from Università Iuav di Venezia with a geopolitical and sociological research and analysis thesis on the European governance of land and sea borders control. From 2018, together with Lorenza Villani, she carries out independent and academic research (research fellowship in 2020 at Iuav) investigating the socio-spatial relationship between immunization, militarization and states of emergency in Europe. She is author of different kinds of publications related to her research field that includes European governance of migration, Italian reception policies, Italian territorial development policies. She is part of the European Horizon 2020 project Welcoming Spaces. She participates in exhibitions (including, 15. Venice Architecture Biennial), in international conferences and academic seminars.

Piersandra Di Matteo is a performing arts theorist, dramaturg, and curator. She is research fellow in the frame of ERC funded project INCOMMON at Università Iuav di Venezia, where she teaches Curating Performing Arts. Her theoretical interests range from contemporary theatre to politics of the voice, from dramaturgy to practices in curating. She has been invited to hold conferences and seminars in international research centres and Universities (Hong Kong, Shanghai, London, Singapore, Montréal, Amsterdam, New York City, Philadelphia, San Paolo). She is Romeo Castellucci's closest theoretical collaborator, working in Europe's foremost theatres, museum and international festivals, among the others Opéra de Paris, Ruhrtriennale, Schaubühne Berlin, Wiener Festwochen, Bayerische Staatsoper, Salzburger Festspiele. She is also collaborating as dramaturg with the Argentine director Lola Arias. She is the artistic curator of Atlas of Transitions Biennale for ERT (2018-2020).

Marco Felicioni is a doctoral candidate at the History of Architecture Department at Università Iuav di Venezia. In 2019, he graduated from Politecnico di Milano with a thesis investigating ludic behaviours and strategies in architectural thinking. Now his research interests have shifted to the Venetian Settecento: at Iuav he's dissecting archival documents in order to reconstruct the various stages and events associated with the construction of the Church of Santa Maria del Rosario in Venice, by the architect Giorgio Massari.

Elena Giacomelli is a post-doctoral researcher at the Department of Sociology and Business Law at Alma Mater Studiorum Università di Bologna. She is now working on environmental change and migration dynamics. She obtained a PhD conducting an ethnographic research on social workers with asylum seekers and refugees. Her research and publications focus on mobility and migration, ethnography and cultural sociology. In 2018 she was a visiting research fellow at the University of the Western Cape (South Africa). In 2016 she took an internship in the Australian Population and Migration Research Center (University of Adelaide). She conducted her Master dissertation in The Philippines, focusing on environmentally-displaced people.

Pierluigi Musarò is associate professor of Sociology at the Department of Sociology and Business Law, Alma Mater Studiorum Università di Bologna, where he teaches modules such as Humanitarian Communication and Media and Security. He is visiting fellow at the London School of Economics and Political Science, research fellow at the Institute for Public Knowledge-New York University, and at Melbourne University. He authored several books and papers on the field of migration, borders, human rights, performing arts, media communication. He is currently principal investigator of several European projects. He is president of the Italian NGO YODA and founding director of IT.A.CÀ_migrants and travelers: Festival of Responsible Tourism.

Lorenza Villani is an architect, researcher and PhD candidate in Sociology and Social Reaserch at the Sociology and Business Law Department Università di Bologna. She studied at the American University of Beirut (Lebanon) in the transdisciplinary Master of Urban Planning Policies and Design and she graduated with full marks and with the right of publication at Università Iuav di Venezia with the research project *PANICO. Letture di campi post 11* settembre which investigates the contemporary securitarian spatialities produced by the proliferation of the state of emergency and exception. She participates in international seminars and exhibitions. She is author of several publications investigating the relationship between immunity dynamics, securitization and militarization in the context of emergency processes. She is part of the European project Perceptions and she takes part in independent and self-organized exhibitions and projects such as Assembramenti and she actively collaborates with NGOs.

Immune Morphologies: Forms
of Militarization and Alliance in
Emergency Processes

Editing: Chiara Davino
and Lorenza Villani

Texts: Malvina Borgherini,
Serena Dambrosio, Chiara
Davino, Piersandra Di
Matteo, Marco Felicioni,
Elena Giacomelli, Pierluigi
Musarò, and Lorenza Villani

Translation and proofreading:
Julius De Michelis

Copyediting:
Malvina Borgherini

Design:
Lorenzo Mason Studio

Typeface: LMS Renato Regular,
Lorenzo Mason Studio

Printing and binding:
Grafiche Veneziane, Venice, Italy

Publisher:
Adriatico Book Club

ISBN: 978-88-945731-1-4
First edition, 2022

Adriatico Book Club
www.adriaticobook.club

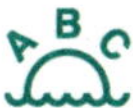

Università Iuav di Venezia
www.iuav.it

I   Università Iuav
---   di Venezia
U

A

V

With kind support of
MeLa Media Lab
www.mela.iuav.it

The project was carried
out within the research
fellowship *Forms of displaying:
analogical supports, digital
platforms and forms of living*
funded by Università Iuav di
Venezia and Associazione
Dimore Storiche Italiane

CO2e emissions for the printing of the book were compensated and neutralised by supporting climate-positive projects.

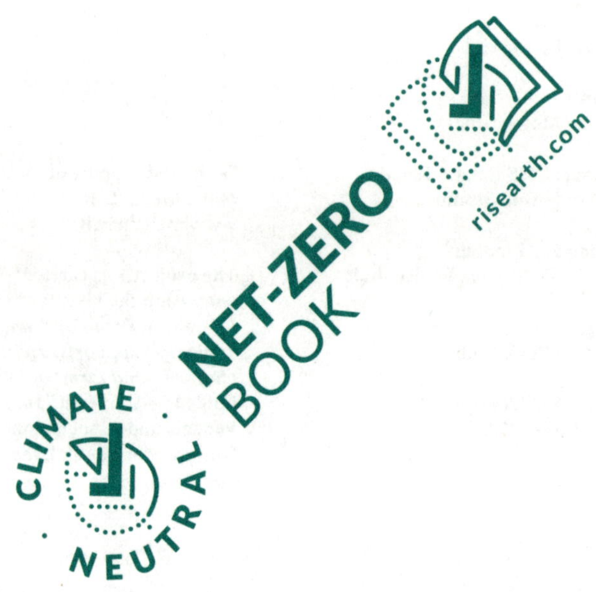